What people are saying about

EXPERIENCING LEADERSHIFT

"What Don Cousins writes, I read. He's among the most insightful church experts in the world. I know from personal experience the joy of being under his leadership. Get out your yellow marker—you're going to have plenty to highlight in his latest contribution."

—LEE STROBEL, AUTHOR OF *THE CASE FOR THE REAL JESUS*

"I've known Don for over thirty years. Without question he is blessed with one of the finest strategic ministry minds in America. I have deeply benefited from his mentoring and friendship. He has served hundreds of leaders on all levels of responsibility, so he knows what he's talking about. If you are a leader, I highly recommend the wisdom in the pages of this book."

—DAN WEBSTER, FOUNDER OF AUTHENTIC LEADERSHIP, INC.

"In my leadership development of thirty thousand leaders over the last twenty-five years I present materials from the most effective communicators in the world. Don Cousins is by far one of the premiere teachers. His profound insight, practicality, and relevance are the best. Follow his advice and your organization will tremendously improve."

—DAN CHUN, COFOUNDER OF HAWAIIAN ISLANDS MINISTRIES AND PASTOR AT FIRST PRESBYTERIAN CHURCH OF HONOLULU

"Books abound that tell pastors how to lead, but this book gives me the tools I have been looking for to raise up faithful and fruitful volunteer leaders in the local church. It is a much-needed resource for those of us who are in the trenches of ministry."

"Don Cousins is a quintessential leader of leaders. He has spoken into my life and into the leadership team of Breakthrough Urban Ministries in ways that have profoundly affected our ministry effectiveness. Those of us who are struggling to see the big picture and to know how to move our organizations forward to excellence need this book."

"As coauthors of *Network*, we have seen over one million believers blessed by an understanding of servanthood and how to use their God-given spiritual gifts and ministry passions. *Experiencing LeaderShift* will be a blessing to the thousands of ministry leaders who have be called to equipped them … but have not yet been equipped to do so."

"Don Cousins' experience with a large number and wide variety of churches has well equipped him to write on contemporary leadership issues. His understanding of the issues has had a tremendous influence on our DMin students, as he has taught for us over the last several years. He has provided a much-needed balance on this subject for churches and church leaders."

"Don Cousins has been a gift to our congregation and to the church here in Hawaii. Through his gifting, expertise, experience, encouragement, and passion, God has used Don in significant ways in helping the church go forth in the Great Commission and in helping the church grow in the Great Commandment. More than anything, Don has been a much-needed coach to many congregations here, and the church in Hawaii is much healthier because of his ministry."

—MARK MORIMOTO, SENIOR PASTOR AT KAKA'AKO CHRISTIAN FELLOWSHIP

"Don Cousins has tapped into a much-needed corrective in leadership development, shifting us back to life-giving truths that will set leaders free. I'm captivated by his biblical vision of leaders becoming the persons God made them to be, learning how to wait patiently for the Lord, and then cooperating with the Spirit's leading, while equipping God's blessed servants to carry out works of service."

—DR. STEPHEN A. MACCHIA, FOUNDER AND PRESIDENT OF LEADERSHIP TRANSFORMATIONS, INC. AND AUTHOR OF BECOMING A HEALTHY TEAM

"Finally someone has written a book that encourages people to be who they are. *Experiencing LeaderShift* brings a life-giving message of correction and encouragement to faithful people tyrannized by soul-damaging myths about leadership. It delivers a powerful combination of relief for the weary and release for the restrained."

—IAN MORGAN CRON, AUTHOR OF CHASING FRANCIS: A PILGRIM'S TALE

As a young pastor given the task of revitalizing an established church, the Lord introduced me to Don Cousins. Don's unique and broad perspective of leadership, coupled with his expertise, insight, and compassion, has made a lasting impact on my shaping as a leader. Don is also an excellent coach, not only in regards to the ministry but to a pastor's personal life as well. I'm not sure where we'd be today if not for Don's influence on our ministry. He is a man of great passion, vision, and integrity, and most of all, a respected friend.

—MIKE KAI, SENIOR PASTOR OF HOPE CHAPEL
WEST O'AHU, WAIKELE, HAWAII.

EXPERIENCING
LEADER*SHIFT*

EXPERIENCING

LEADERSHIFT

LETTING GO
OF LEADERSHIP
HERESIES

DON COUSINS

David C Cook®
transforming lives together

EXPERIENCING LEADERSHIFT
Published by David C. Cook
4050 Lee Vance View
Colorado Springs, CO 80918 U.S.A.

David C. Cook Distribution Canada
55 Woodslee Avenue, Paris, Ontario, Canada N3L 3E5

David C. Cook U.K., Kingsway Communications
Eastbourne, East Sussex BN23 6NT, England

David C. Cook and the graphic circle C logo
are registered trademarks of Cook Communications Ministries.

The Web site addresses recommended throughout this book are offered as a resource to
you. These Web sites are not intended in any way to be or imply an endorsement on the
part of David C. Cook, nor do we vouch for their content.

Unless otherwise indicated, Scripture quotations are from the *New American Standard Bible* © 1960, 1995 by
The Lockman Foundation. Used by Permission. Other Scripture quotations are from the *Holy Bible, New
International Version,® NIV®* (NIV) © 1973, 1978, 1984 by International Bible Society. Used by permission of
Zondervan. Italics in Scripture quotations are the author's emphasis.

LCCN 2008922169
Hardcover ISBN 978-1-4347-6854-4
International Trade Paperback ISBN 978-1-4347-6833-9

© 2008 Don Cousins
Published in association with the Literary agency of Wolgemuth & Associates, Inc.

The Team: Terry Behimer, Thomas Womack, Jaci Schneider, Karen Athen
Cover Design: The DesignWorks Group, David Uttley
Interior Design: The DesignWorks Group

Printed in the United States of America
First Edition 2008

1 2 3 4 5 6 7 8 9 10

020408

To those who serve the body of Christ
by providing leadership:

May you lead from the zone of God's anointing and
experience smashing success

CONTENTS

ACKNOWLEDGMENTS

How blessed I have been to work with the team at David C. Cook. In particular I wish to thank Terry Behimer, Ryan Dunham, Cris Doornbos, Don Pape, Dan Rich, Jaci Schneider, Mike Kennedy, Kate Amaya, and Denise Washington. They have demonstrated a heart for God, a passion to see His truth proclaimed, and a competence in their respective roles that has provided me with the best possible publishing experience.

I want to thank Thomas Womack, whose editorial efforts reflect God's anointing, and as a result, have significantly improved this book.

Robert and Erik Wolgemuth—whose contribution is most simply described with the words "skillful servants"—provide proof once again that great skill, combined with a servant's heart, make for a powerful one-two punch.

Bruce Bugbee—a brother, fellow worker, and fellow soldier, whose life and ministry reflect his commitment to gift-based, passion-driven ministry—offered many valuable suggestions to this book.

Charlie Halley is the embodiment of an equipping leader.

Nancy VanDyke—who possesses the gift of interpretation … to read my writing, that is—did an outstanding job of typing my manuscript, with an attitude that made her a joy to work with.

And thanks to those whose experiences serve as illustrations in this book. While I've changed their names, their stories remain true.

Most of all, I am indebted to my family: to my mother, Jean Cousins, whose example caused me to want to follow Jesus and whose prayers on my behalf have yielded more fruit than either she or I will perhaps ever know; to my children, Kyle, Kirk, and Karalyne—living examples and daily reminders of God's grace toward me; to MaryAnn, my partner, who has been asked to make many shifts of her own as a result of being married to me. Her unwavering commitment to the Lord and me has played a bigger role in my ability to write what I have than she will ever know.

PART ONE

A Departure from Truth

1

LEADERSHIP HERESIES

A story is told of a young man filling out his college application. One of the questions on the form read, "Are you a leader or a follower?" He checked "follower."

A few weeks later the dean telephoned him. "I don't normally call students to congratulate them on their acceptance to our college," he said. "But in your case, we're particularly glad to have you. We've accepted five hundred students for the coming year—499 of whom identify themselves as leaders."

Recently, as I was preparing to teach on the topic of "following," I went to a nearby Barnes & Noble to do a little research. At the help desk I asked the attendant how many titles the store carried on the topic of leadership. She checked the computer and quickly found 125, telling me they probably carried more. Then I asked how many titles they carried on the topic of "followership."

A puzzled look came across her face. "Followership?"

"Yes," I answered. "Leaders need followers, right? I want to know how many books you carry that could help someone become a great follower."

She turned back to her computer and searched for several minutes. "Two," she said.

I was pleasantly surprised, as I hadn't expected to find any. But my surprise quickly turned to disappointment when she told me the titles of the two books, each of which included the word *leadership*. Both books were written for leaders and focused on leadership issues—I'd already read one of them. Each made only a brief mention of the role of followers.

Why do we place such an emphasis on the topic of leadership? It seems everyone likes to think of himself or herself as a leader—and wants to be considered a leader by others. No one, it seems, wants to be called a follower. Leadership is where it's at.

Missing the Gift

Pastor David and I had stopped for lunch after he picked me up at the airport. A brief visit would give us time to get acquainted before I met with the church's leadership team.

The church David had planted a year earlier had gotten off to a strong start but now struggled to break through the two-hundred barrier in weekly attendance. After we discussed his spiritual gifts, David hung his head. "I don't have the gift of leadership," he confessed. "I don't know if I can build a great church."

Seeing his discouragement, I reached for my Bible and asked him, "Show me where it states, 'You must have the spiritual gift of leadership to build a great church.'"

He quickly acknowledged he knew of no such passage.

"How about where it states, 'You need the gift of leadership to lead a church, even a church that isn't so great'?"

Again, he was unaware of any such Scripture.

"Then where," I asked him, "did you get the impression you need to possess the spiritual gift of leadership to build a great church?"

"It seems like every conference I attend and every book I read tells me I need to be a great leader," he answered. "Leadership, leadership, leadership—that's all I seem to hear about. I guess I've concluded it's a necessary gift if you want to build a church."

David's not alone in his conclusion. Several years ago a Barna Group survey indicated that only 8 percent of America's pastors see themselves as having the spiritual gift of leadership—a troubling statistic indeed if you attend the conferences and read the books David has. Most of these books and conferences bear a "leadership" label and are aimed at producing stronger leaders.

I've coached enough pastors among the 92 percent to know that many have reached the same conclusion as my friend David, and they share the same disappointment. It doesn't take long to become convinced that becoming a great leader is the key to success. Success is based on your ability to lead. If you have "the gift," you have a promising future. If you don't, then start attending every leadership conference and start reading every leadership book you can get a hold of—because if God didn't make you a "gifted leader," you've got to make yourself one.

The same Barna survey taken today might bring different results—not because facts have changed, but because of the deep desire to see them change. I've found that a significant percentage of that 92 percent have talked themselves into believing they possess "the gift" (as typically defined). They want it, and their churches want it for them, so *not* having it is something few are willing to confess. In today's culture it seems easier to admit being an addict of some kind. Perhaps we need to start support groups for those who acknowledge they aren't "gifted leaders": "Hi, my name is Bob, and I don't have the spiritual gift of leadership." That admission is more than the average ego can take. As a result the "non-gifted" work very hard to become better leaders and overcome the Holy Spirit's "distribution error" in failing to gift them appropriately.

This misplaced emphasis on the spiritual gift of leadership has damaged the hearts and minds of many who fill positions of leadership. It has skewed their understanding of their role and contribution, and the distorting effects have been widely felt among those they lead. Churches and ministries have suffered.

This is why I'm suggesting that we need to let go of leadership heresies. I'm referring to the broad definition of *heresy*: "an error, a lie, a mistake in belief." Heresies reflect a mixture of truth and error that alter God's intended message and desired outcome. In the end heresies lead astray those who believe in them, bringing consequences that inevitably result from any departure from God's truth.

Such is the case here. Leadership is important—critically important, but believing that leadership is the most important or most needed gift is heretical. It's also heretical to believe that leadership's expression is limited to just one gift.

In our culture, people place a great deal of emphasis and value on SNLs (strong natural leaders), while the church emphasizes and values the "gifted leader." The concept is essentially the same, but the language is modified to make it sound more spiritual. Such an emphasis in the church is not a reflection of Scripture but of worldly philosophy and practice, and the results have done more harm than good.

Getting Our Biblical Facts Straight

The Bible simply doesn't state that those in positions of leadership should seek the spiritual gift of leadership. In fact none of the New Testament writers tells anyone to pursue it.

So what *should* we seek? Paul writes, "Pursue love, yet desire earnestly spiritual gifts, but especially that you may prophesy" (1 Cor. 14:1). If you want to pursue any gift as *the* gift, Paul says, make it prophecy. Communicating revelation from God is at the top of the list. If we really took Paul's words to heart, we would be holding and attending more prophecy conferences, right? And my pastor friend David would be more concerned about lacking *this* gift than that of leadership.

Nowhere in 1 Corinthians 12, 13, or 14 is the word *leadership* even mentioned. Neither is it found in Ephesians 4 or 1 Peter 4, other key passages on spiritual gifts. In fact, in the primary passages on the gifts, the *only* mention of leadership is Romans 12:8, which exhorts "he who leads" to do so "with diligence." If the spiritual gift of leadership were as indispensable as some would have us believe, then the apostles would have placed more emphasis on it than those five words—"he who leads, with diligence." Truth is, in reading the passages on spiritual gifts, we find that the writers barely mention the gift of leadership.

One could make the case that the focus of Romans 12:8 is not so much on the gift of leadership as it is on the need for diligence by anyone occupying a leadership position. I realize that some liken the gift of leadership to that of apostleship mentioned in 1 Corinthians 12:28 and Ephesians 4:11. But if we want to make those two gifts synonymous, we should refer to the gift of leadership as the gift of apostleship.

I do believe some possess the spiritual gift of leadership. But touting it as *the* all-important, absolutely needed, indispensable gift for those in positions of leadership is not in accordance with biblical truth. This erroneous belief has had several damaging effects:

1. God's wisdom and sovereignty in the distribution of gifts is questioned.

Paul tells us in 1 Corinthians 12:11 that the Holy Spirit distributes the gifts "to each one individually just as He wills." *We* don't select our spiritual gifts; the Spirit does. If, in fact, 92 percent of America's pastors are not "gifted leaders," yet we insist that such giftedness is necessary, we can't escape the notion that the Holy Spirit has left the body of Christ short.

While none of us wants to call into question God's wisdom and sovereignty, this is essentially what we're doing. It gives rise to a spirit of dissatisfaction with who God made us to be and how He has gifted us. How often I hear a pastor or ministry leader say, "I wish I were a stronger leader." Any time we exalt a specific gift as supremely important, those who don't possess it are tempted to complain: "God, You didn't give *me* what is central to *my* success."

But such grumbling is sin and needs to be confessed as such. It needs to be repented of. To believe the Holy Spirit makes *any* error, in distribution or otherwise, is a lie and results in bondage for the one who thinks that way. The truth is, the Holy Spirit bestows all our gifts "just as He wills." That includes *your* gifts. So rejoice in that truth, and serve in freedom and power accordingly.

2. The placement of "non-gifted" leaders in ministry is questioned.

If 92 percent of America's pastors don't possess the gift of leadership, yet occupy positions of leadership in their churches, then they must be mis-slotted. Maybe the Holy Spirit didn't make a distribution error, but many of His servants must have made an application error.

I know, from firsthand experience, the number of pastors who struggle with their supposed lack of leadership giftedness. "Can I still pastor this church?" they ask. "Has the church outgrown my ability to lead it? Do they need someone more gifted than me?"

They're also confused about what leadership looks like on a day-to-day basis. "What should I be doing? What's my role? What priorities should I be focusing on?" I hear these questions all the time. They come not only from leaders but also from team members who serve under their influence. "How can we help our pastor become a better leader? Can he even lead our church? Or do we need a different leader altogether?"

So the right slot in ministry is a point of both internal and external tension for the "non-gifted" leader.

While I would agree that some who occupy positions of leadership are serving outside their gifting, the percentage isn't as high as 92 percent. Ninety-two percent did not make a mistake when they followed what they believed to be God's leading into their current roles.

We must stop bombarding ourselves with questions of competence that serve only to undermine our confidence. While there's a time to thoughtfully and prayerfully consider your role in ministry, you can't do that all the time. I'm fully in favor of prayerful examination of your role in ministry. I enthusiastically approve of your gaining input from godly counselors who love you. If such an appraisal suggests a major change, make it. If it suggests a minor adjustment, adjust. If neither, then move ahead with the confidence that God has you right where He wants you.

3. Those leading try to become like someone else, rather than remaining true to who they are.

It should come as no surprise that leadership conferences are usually put on by those who score high for the gift of leadership. Books on leadership are written either by these same "gifted" leaders or by people who study their practices. That's because today's church, just like our culture, places SNLs / "gifted leaders" on a pedestal. We've made mini-gods out of them. We stand in awe of the organizations and churches they've built. People tell their stories over and over and study and record their habits. And the message is clear: Think as they think, relate as they relate, make decisions as they make them. By all means do as they do … and you, too, can be a great leader just like them.

Recently a pastor told me about attending a conference led by one of these "gifted leaders." At the conclusion this leader stood before his audience and told them unashamedly that the best thing they could do to become better leaders was to buy his books and videos.

Some are buying this message and trying to remake themselves and their ministries in the image of a gifted leader. Rather than focusing their efforts and energy on developing and using the gifts God has given them, they focus on becoming like someone else.

Trying to minister out of someone else's gifting is a huge mistake. I observed this firsthand while on staff at Willow Creek Community Church. Curious pastors from all over the country came to find out what was responsible for our "success" (numerical growth). Many pastors returned home from our conferences (called Church Leadership Conferences) committed to launching seeker services in an effort to trigger conversion growth in their church. While their intentions for doing so were good, their implementations and results often were not.

Some sought to copy everything we did. One pastor called to ask what paper stock and ink we used for the bulletin. Another sought permission to copy the church logo. I know of pastors who even gave replica sermons from Willow Creek, including illustrations.

I'd like to believe that if God wanted us to mimic a particular strategy for building His church, He would have put that strategy in His Word. *We've made the mistake of trying to copy the methodology of "success" rather than the process behind the methodology.* The ministry strategy Willow Creek employed is not the key to the church's high growth rate. The growth occurred for various reasons: The Holy Spirit released His anointing in the area of evangelism, church leaders cooperated with the Spirit's movement by employing a strategy that assisted this spirit of evangelism, and roles and contributions reflected each individual's gifts and passions. As a result the power of God was at work.

Programming methodologies come and go as time passes and cultures change. But the Spirit's anointing and our need to cooperate with Him are timeless.

Be the person God made you to be. Let your service flow from the gifts God has given you. Cooperate with the Holy Spirit's movement in your ministry. As Henry Blackaby has written in *Experiencing God,* "Find out where God is at work and join Him." Identify God's activity in your world and become part of what you see. God wants to do new works. Just take a look at the world around you and see the expanse of His creativity.

To learn from others is great! Trying to become like them is not.

4. Those with the gift of leadership are prevented from exercising their gift.

Perspectives differ concerning the number of spiritual gifts. Some people believe there are only nine, corresponding in number to the fruit of the Spirit listed in Galatians 5:22–23 and limited to the list given in 1 Corinthians 12:8–10. Others believe the number is far greater than nine and includes gifts not even mentioned in the New Testament passages on spiritual gifts.

For a number of reasons, I'm part of this second group (though this isn't a matter of doctrine over which I would fight to the death). Several years ago, when Bruce Bugbee, Bill Hybels, and I compiled the content for *Network* (a curriculum focused on spiritual gifts), we reflected this position. We defined and described the spiritual gift of leadership as "the divine enablement to cast vision, motivate, and direct people to harmoniously accomplish the purposes of God." We went on to write,

People with this gift …

- provide direction for God's people in ministry.
- motivate others to perform to the best of their abilities.
- present the "big picture" for others to see.
- model the values of the ministry.
- take responsibility and establish goals.

People with this gift tend to be … influential, diligent, visionary, trustworthy, persuasive, motivating, and goal-setting.

While I have no desire to argue whether what we described is, in fact, a spiritual gift, I would argue strongly that such people do exist. Some folks, by God's design, fit the above description to a tee. I call these people "organization builders." When they do their thing, they build an organization. I believe this is Barna's 8 percent, those who score high for the gift of leadership. And just as the church needs gifted teachers and gifted evangelists, it also needs gifted leaders. We need organization builders because the church functions as an organization.

I've found from experience that these gifted leaders (organization builders) have the God-given ability to perform four necessary tasks:

1. They build a staff—a team of workers.

2. They formulate strategies whereby ministry is carried out.

3. They design the structure whereby everyone has a role to fill and a contribution to make.

4. They create systems allowing the staff to implement the strategies within the designed structures.

Organization builders do all this naturally, just as teachers capture and communicate truth naturally and evangelists share the gospel naturally.

After more than thirty years in ministry, fifteen of which I've spent coaching Christian leaders and organizations, my opinion is that most pastors are *not* organization builders by God's design. I believe the Barna survey supports that conclusion. It's also my opinion that the organization builders are the ones who put on the conferences and write the books conveying the importance of leadership. This should come as a surprise to no one; they see the world through the lens of an organization-building leader.

This is called "gift projection." Because someone sees ministry through his particular gifting, he projects his gifting onto others. It's difficult for the organization builder to understand why others can't see things as he or she does.

As a nineteen-year-old freshman in college, I took a spiritual gifts inventory for the first time. I scored highest for the gift of leadership. In that moment I understood why I enjoyed and prospered in leadership roles: God was working through me in that area. Building teams, formulating strategies, designing structures, and creating systems is what I love to do—by God's design. But for years I couldn't understand why others didn't enjoy these activities as I did. I would grow frustrated and become critical of those who were less than successful in team-building or strategy formulation. I know I was guilty of gift projection. And I know my frustration and criticism brought hurt to those whose gifting differed from mine.

It's not that it's wrong for any of us to emphasize our areas of gifting. When I listen to Billy Graham, I expect an emphasis on evangelism. And when an organization builder speaks, I expect the focus to be leadership.

The thing is, organization builders tend to build bigger churches and ministries because building things is what they do, by God's anointing. And because we're impressed by BIG, we go to them to learn all we can so we, too, can become BIG. The trouble is, the vast majority of pastors (92 percent, if the survey was accurate) are *not* designed or anointed as organization builders, a.k.a. "gifted leaders." But because we expect them to be, we also see this fourth effect, perhaps the most damaging of all: *Those who possess the spiritual gift of leadership are prevented from exercising their gift.*

Take my friend Brian, a businessman who serves as an elder at his church. He creates a following wherever he goes. He has a vision for the things he's involved in and naturally communicates that vision to those he relates to. He's clearly going somewhere.

And not only is he going somewhere, he also has a plan for how to get there. People see this movement in his life and inevitably want to get on board.

Brian thinks strategically. He has a knack for gathering the resources he needs to accomplish his goals. He's a team builder who understands people and how to get the best out of them in ways they enjoy. Brian obviously has the spiritual gift of leadership.

While he believes God has called him to the marketplace, Brian is also very committed to both his church and several parachurch ministries. On more than one occasion over the dozen years we've known each other, he has said to me, "My pastor is going to drive me crazy. He just doesn't get it." Brian loves his pastor and is deeply committed to supporting him, but he also recognizes that his pastor doesn't possess the gift of leadership. Yes, he's an anointed *teacher* and a wonderful *pastor*—he's just not an organization builder. It's hard for him to put the church's vision into words. He isn't even clear on what the vision is. He doesn't think in strategic ways and can't seem to put a plan in place. While he's really good with people, he doesn't really know how to lead them in a way that brings forth the best from them. Calling the church staff a "team" would be an exaggeration. They operate more as employees of an organization than they do as teammates committed to a common vision.

Brian isn't troubled by the fact that his pastor's not an organization builder. He appreciates who his pastor is. Brian's struggle is with the fact that the pastor feels obligated to be *the* leader, thereby preventing more qualified people from bringing their leadership skills to bear on the life of the church. Brian would be happy to help the church capture its vision on paper and to craft a plan to make the vision a reality. He would be thrilled to help assemble a team to lead in implementing the strategy. But Brian's influence is limited. The very person who most wants him to be committed to the work of his church—the pastor—is stifling him.

As a result Brian invests his prime leadership energy in the marketplace and helps out in the church only when called upon. I know Brian, his pastor, and the church well enough to say that Brian is giving—and the church receiving—only a portion of what Brian has to offer.

Laypeople who possess the spiritual gift of leadership represent a huge untapped resource in the church today. What do we do with them? How can we best use what they have to offer? How do we employ their gifting to help build the Kingdom of God? This will be a dilemma as long as we hang on to the model that says the pastor must be responsible for building and leading the organization. Truly great leaders understand their need to go beyond themselves as they work to fulfill their organization's mission.

Those pastors who are not gifted leaders (organization builders) need to learn how to fully utilize those around them who *are* such leaders. You require no special skill to surround yourself with such people—only a measure of personal security and the willingness to give up some control. (In later chapters I'll discuss how pastors can fulfill their role in keeping with their design while delegating organization-building to others.)

People like my friend Brian fill the Kingdom of God. They're waiting to be called upon to use what God has given them so they might be faithful, fruitful, and fulfilled in a ministry that makes God famous. Since they're gifted to lead, we need to *let* them lead.

But for this to become a reality, our cultural understanding of leadership requires a paradigm shift to one that is more biblical. Gifting and anointing *must* outweigh title and position in importance.

A Biblical Understanding of Leadership

There's no question that leadership is a critical issue in any endeavor. A great deal of truth rests in the saying "Everything rises and falls on leadership." Equal truth is in the statement "Speed of the leader, speed of the team." Strong, effective leadership makes a big difference. But at the same time, our understanding of leadership must be shaped by biblical truth, not by worldly philosophies and practices. And we must follow these in order for us and our work to prosper.

Biblical Truth 1: Leadership is expressed in different ways through a variety of gifts.

The expression of leadership isn't limited to one spiritual gift called "leadership." Note specifically what Paul writes in each of these two consecutive verses:

> And He gave some as apostles, and some as prophets, and some as evangelists, and some as pastors and teachers.... (Eph. 4:11)

... for the equipping of the saints for the work of
service, to the building up of the body of Christ.
(4:12)

In verse 11 Paul lists five spiritual gifts, all having what I call a
leadership effect—providing leadership to those on the receiving
end:

- The apostle *leads* through the launching of a new work.
- The prophet *leads* by bringing a message that edifies and
  exhorts.
- The evangelist *leads* by proclaiming the gospel to those who
  aren't yet saved.
- The pastor *leads* by shepherding a group of people.
- The teacher *leads* by providing instruction from the Word.

All five belong under the heading "leadership gifts," since
they cannot be used without first having people who follow.
And while each gift is expressed differently, the result for all is
the same (in verse 12): Followers are equipped for the work of
service. If those with these gifts do not equip the saints for the
work of service, then they are not using these gifts as God
intended.

Ed pastors a church with a Sunday morning attendance of
two thousand, but he lacks the spiritual gift of leadership (or at
least he scores low in "leadership" on various spiritual gift
assessments). He's quick to say, "I like the church staff, but I'd
just as soon not attend staff meetings." Ed isn't a meeting guy.

He's not a vision, mission, or strategy guy either. While he appreciates these organizational realities and affirms their importance, he doesn't want to agonize over their formulation or implementation.

Ed is a teacher. Teaching is his spiritual gift. His joy is in the study and presentation of God's Word, and for the past twenty years he has spent thirty hours each week studying to present God's Word in life-changing ways to his congregation. As a teacher Ed is doing what God gifted him to do. And through this anointing he has led his church to a place of prevailing influence within his community. Ed leads through his teaching gift. To say Ed is not a leader is ridiculous.

I could tell you dozens of stories of pastors who've led effectively *without* the gift of leadership. It would be a big mistake to tell them they're missing a critical piece for effectiveness because they don't possess "the gift." It would be an equal shame to tell Ed he needs to start attending multiple meetings so he can play a greater role in forming and implementing ministry vision, mission, and strategy. Such direction would lead him outside his gifting. His participation in such meetings would probably only frustrate those who are truly skilled with such matters.

Please understand, I'm not saying that Ed should be permanently excused from staff meetings and strategy sessions. As the primary communicator to his congregation, it's essential that he understand and uphold the church's strategic direction. He plays a critical role in equipping the body of Christ to carry out the identified strategy. But he needs to do this out of *his* gifting. And when he does it in tandem with an organization builder, together they deliver a powerful one-two punch.

Leadership, biblically defined, expresses itself through *different* spiritual gifts. Experience tells me that many of those 92 percent who don't score high for "the gift" are still leaders. They simply provide leadership through the gifts they possess, whether apostleship, prophecy, evangelism, pastoring, or teaching.

Biblical Truth 2: The expression of biblically defined leadership results in the equipping of others for the work of service.

Dale Galloway is credited with saying, "A true leader is not someone who can do the work of ten people, but someone who can organize ten people to do the work." This is what Paul had in mind when he wrote those two verses in Ephesians 4. Look at them again:

> (11) And He gave some as apostles, and some as prophets, and some as evangelists, and some as pastors and teachers, (12) for the equipping of the saints for the work of service, to the building up of the body of Christ.

Biblically expressed leadership brings this result: "the equipping of the saints for the work of service." *If you hold a leadership position but are not equipping the saints for the work of service, then you are not a leader.* You may hold the position; you may have the title; you may be *called* a leader; but you're not a leader as the Bible defines it, because leadership means equipping.

As a leader your role, your responsibility, your contribution, and your calling is to equip ten people to do the work. If *you* are doing the work of those ten people, then you're not a leader; you're a server.

Looking back at Paul's words in Ephesians 4, a leader makes a verse-11 contribution to the body of Christ. And the fruit of that verse-11 contribution is seen in the evidence described in verse 12: The saints are equipped for the work of service in building up the body.

This definition and description of leadership didn't start with Paul. We can go all the way back to Moses and his father-in-law, Jethro. Remember what a wise old man Jethro was?

> Moses' father-in-law said to him, "The thing that you are doing is not good. You will surely wear out, both yourself and these people who are with you, for the task is too heavy for you; you cannot do it alone. Now listen to me: I will give you counsel, and God be with you. You be the people's representative before God, and you bring the disputes to God, then teach them the statutes and the laws, and make known to them the way in which they are to walk and the work they are to do. Furthermore, you shall select out of all the people able men who fear God, men of truth, those who hate dishonest gain; and you shall place these over them as leaders of thousands, of hundreds, of fifties and of tens. Let them judge the people at all times; and let it be that every major dispute they will bring to you, but every minor dispute they themselves will judge. So it will be easier for you, and they will bear the burden with you.

If you do this thing and God so commands you, then you will be able to endure, and all these people also will go to their place in peace."

So Moses listened to his father-in-law and did all that he had said. Moses chose able men out of all Israel and made them heads over the people, leaders of thousands, of hundreds, of fifties and of tens. They judged the people at all times; the difficult dispute they would bring to Moses, but every minor dispute they themselves would judge.

Then Moses bade his father-in-law farewell, and he went his way into his own land. (Ex. 18:17–27)

Prior to Jethro's instructions, Moses (to put it in Ephesians 4 terms) was in a verse-11 position but busy with verse-12 efforts. That's when Jethro told him, "The thing that you are doing is not good." We could say the same to all those in leadership positions (verse-11 roles) who function as servers (verse-12 roles). The Holy Spirit has distributed gifts such that the body of Christ has the exact number of verse-11 people and the exact number of verse-12 people needed to make the church function as God desires.

While I was at Willow Creek, it became clear we needed to add more manpower in pastoral care as the church and the surrounding community kept growing. Ministering to the sick, the grieving, and the hurting was an important and valued ministry, and the number of such people coming our way for help was increasing. So we hired a man—I'll call him Sam—who'd been a pastor for a number of years and possessed strong gifting in mercy and encouragement. He was a true man of God, of highest integrity, with the heart of God for those who hurt. He seemed like a perfect choice to be director of pastoral care.

From the onset, even in the interview process, we made it clear we were looking for Sam to identify and equip an army of mercy givers. Considering the size of the church body, the population of the community, and the fact that four major hospitals were within driving distance of the church, we would *need* an army to meet the existing needs. Sam said he understood his role as an equipper.

About eighteen months later we had to transition Sam off the church staff. Why? We never questioned his heart for God, his love for people, or his integrity. But he was more a mercy giver than he was an *equipper* of mercy givers. He was never fully able to identify—or equip—an army. Given the choice between ministering mercy and encouragement to someone in the hospital and conducting a training session for twenty-five mercy givers, he would go to the hospital. And that was okay—it was who God made him to be. He was in the right place when he sat with a patient or a family grieving the loss of a loved one. Compassion poured from his heart at such times. He wasn't at fault when his new staff position didn't work out; we were. We'd hired a person with a verse-12 gifting and focus when we needed someone with a verse-11 gifting and focus.

This isn't to say verse-11 and verse-12 people are mutually exclusive. No one is *only* verse 11 or *only* verse 12. But by our gifting we're primarily one or the other. For Sam it wasn't that he *never* selected anyone for his army of mercy; he did. And it wasn't that he hadn't trained *anyone;* he did train a few. It's that he desired to focus on providing pastoral care personally, while we needed a leader of pastoral care whose gifting was more in equipping others to extend mercy.

Shortly after Sam's departure we hired a man out of the marketplace who fit the position perfectly. Like Sam he had a passion for the hurting, but he was primarily an equipper. He had started and built a social services agency, and as a result was experienced in providing services to those in need. At Willow Creek he ended up building an army of mercy givers whose influence for Christ in the church and community was momentous.

I learned a very important biblical lesson in the process: Those in leadership positions *must focus* their ministry on equipping others for the work of service. Not because they're told to, but because that's what God has designed them to do. An equipping ministry needs to reflect God's gifting in one's life; I equip others for the work of service not because I hold a leadership position, but because that's what God equipped me to do.

This is the way God has structured the body of Christ. Leaders equip servers, who in turn do the work of service. The results of this design are spelled out in the continuing verses in Ephesians 4:

> ... until we all attain to the unity of the faith, and of the knowledge of the Son of God, to a mature man, to the measure of the stature which belongs to the fullness of Christ. As a result, we are no longer to be children, tossed here and there by waves and carried about by every wind of doctrine, by the trickery of men, by craftiness in deceitful scheming; but speaking the truth in

love, we are to grow up in all aspects into Him who is
the head, even Christ, from whom the whole body,
being fitted and held together by what every joint supplies, according to the proper working of each individual
part, causes the growth of the body for the building up
of itself in love. (4:13–16)

While this information may not be new for many church and
ministry leaders, I've found a gap between knowledge and application. We're familiar with the concept of equipping found in
Ephesians 4:11–12, but the way we lead doesn't reflect that truth.

Let's do it. Let's shape our leadership to function according to biblical truth. When we do, the results will speak for themselves.

Summary

Leadership is a critical component in any endeavor. A great deal of
truth rests in the statements "Everything rises and falls on leadership" and "Speed of the leader, speed of the team."

So with only 8 percent of pastors scoring high for having "leadership" as a primary gift—did the Holy Spirit commit a distribution
error in His gifts to the church? Obviously not! Have 92 percent of
the pastors currently filling positions of leaders made an application
error as it relates to the role they play? I don't think so.

This leaves only one explanation for those percentages being
okay as they are: God's definition of leadership and His understanding of leadership are different than ours. We've allowed
worldly philosophy and practice concerning leadership to infiltrate

the church. We've embraced mistaken notions and become confused about the nature and function of leadership in the body of
Christ.

We need to experience a leadershift—*a return to a biblical definition and understanding of leadership that functions as God intended.*

While the body of Christ needs the gift of leadership, it is not
the most important or most needed gift—even for those in positions of leadership. In addition, leadership is expressed through
more gifts than just one.

We need to stop questioning the wisdom and sovereignty of God
in the distribution of spiritual gifts. We need to stop beating ourselves
up for who we are *not*. We need to start thanking God and worship-
ping Him for His perfect wisdom and understanding that gave each of
us the gifts He wanted us to have.

We need to stop telling those who score low for the gift of "leadership" that they can't be leaders in the church. We need to start
encouraging those with other leadership gifts to develop and use
them to provide leadership in accordance with their gifting.

We need to stop the practice of gift projection that conveys the
message, "Without the gift of leadership, you can't be an effective
leader—you can't build a great church." We need to exercise discernment whenever we hear someone say, "Become a leader like me."

We need to start releasing those with the gift of leadership
(organization builders) to use their gift in the life of the church. We
need to allow laypeople with this gift to be the organization
builders God made them to be. We need to stop doing the work of
ten people and focus instead on equipping ten people to do the
work. Those in positions of leadership need to stop functioning as
trained servers and start functioning as equipping leaders.

We need to stop seeking to emulate the SNLs that the world holds up as the ideal image. We need to embrace the truth of God's Word in its definition and understanding of leadership.

We need to experience a leadershift.

In fact we need to make a number of leadershifts. In doing so, we'll let go of some of the leadership heresies that have made their way into the church. In the pages ahead I'll seek to identify additional heresies that are affecting leaders in the church today. We need to overcome them—lest the story and facts you see in the next chapter become a recurring pattern.

2

THE HIGH PRICE OF HERESY

After seventeen years of nonstop ministry, I was completely exhausted. *How can I be so tired,* I thought, *yet have such a hard time sleeping? Why must I struggle now to muster motivation, when I have always been highly motivated? How can I feel so spiritually empty when I'm doing everything I'm supposed to do to be filled?* I just couldn't summon the energy to battle any longer. In spite of disciplined efforts to avoid it, I was flirting with burnout. I'd hit a wall—physically run down, emotionally strung out, mentally fatigued, and spiritually empty.

I felt as though I were dying inside. And while I took great comfort in Jesus' invitation, "Come to Me, all who are weary and heavy-laden, and I will give you rest," I was troubled by His next words: "Take My yoke upon you.... *For My yoke is easy and My burden is light*" (Matt. 11:28–30). Really? *Easy? Light?* To me His yoke seemed hard, and His load was killing me! Something was broken and in desperate need of being fixed.

Unshakable Restlessness

A nagging restlessness about my ministry at Willow Creek compounded my troubled condition. For the better part of eighteen months, I'd sensed that my ministry with the church was coming to an end. I tried to ignore and even silence the distress. After all, what logical sense did it make to leave the staff of one of the most effective and respected churches in America? I'd helped plant Willow Creek in the fall of 1975 and spent nearly two decades working hard to help bring it to where it was. By all visible indication, the ministry, and my involvement in it, were marked by smashing success. Some 15,000 people regularly attended weekend services. Full-time staff numbered 175, with another 175 part-time. We had nearly a hundred internal ministries, most with flourishing numbers. And we'd just completed a major building expansion that would enable us to take the church's ministry to new levels of growth and development.

It made no sense to leave, especially since I had a wife and three children to support. I had a sufficient salary, a generous benefits package, a nice office, a great staff, and the respect of the Willow community. The days of no pay, no benefits, no office, and no vacation were long gone. Yet the restlessness I felt was impossible to silence or ignore.

Pride prevented me from confessing I was struggling. A couple of months away might mean the difference between survival and burnout, but to request a break seemed like an admission of weakness—and what could be worse than that? If the church granted my request, what about the guilt I would no doubt feel?

To me, "paid time off" was an oxymoron. And what if my request was denied?

Maybe this explained why I wasn't sleeping well. Stress had begun to take a toll. I *needed* the break. So I finally asked.

The elders at Willow Creek graciously granted my request to get away for a while. They gave me a four-month sabbatical to rest, recharge my batteries, and listen for God's direction. And to the degree that it's possible to accomplish those things with children ages five, three, and one, I did.

For my wife, MaryAnn, it wasn't an easy place to be—having three little kids and a worn-out husband unsure if he would keep his job. Though we spent considerable time together as a family, she also gave me the freedom to spend large blocks of time with God, with spiritual mentors, and with close friends.

My First Question

To describe my time off as "R & R" would give a false impression, because two questions in particular weighed heavily on me, keeping me preoccupied by day and tossing sleeplessly by night.

The first question: *What is it, God, that You want me to do?* It seemed I asked that a hundred times a day. And I had only four months to get an answer. I couldn't in good conscience return to Willow Creek with anything less than a clear leading from God. Eighteen years earlier a clear leading had moved me from the athletic world to the ministry. A clear leading also placed me with Bill Hybels and a few others in planting Willow Creek shortly thereafter. For all those years I'd sensed I was where God wanted me to be. But was I now? I was sensing strongly that the answer was no, but I didn't want to make a huge decision—affecting not only me, but my entire family—based on a "sense." I wanted unmistakable direction. I wanted a *mandate*. And if I wasn't going to continue at Willow Creek, what *was* I going to do?

So over and over I asked God what He wanted me to do, and waited intently for His answer. I listened for God's guiding voice in every reading of His Word, in every prayer time, in every experience and circumstance, and in each conversation with a family member, friend, or spiritual mentor.

Looking back, I realize that in itself, my intense pursuit of God's direction fulfilled what He wanted:

> "For I know the plans that I have for you," declares the LORD, "plans for welfare and not for calamity to give you a future and a hope. Then you will call upon Me ... and *I will listen to you*. You will seek Me and find Me *when you search for Me with all your heart*." (Jer. 29:11–13)

He allows, and even causes, circumstances that press us to search for Him with all our hearts. I was in such a circumstance. And while God seemed at times to be a million miles away, He was, in fact, quite near. He'd let me reach the end of myself for a reason. Without realizing it, my batteries were recharging as I searched wholeheartedly for Him. He was renewing my spirit even as I sought Him for an answer to my question.

I now know that my goal and God's goal were different. I wanted an answer to my question; God wanted *me*. I was all about the product; He was all about the process. I was focused on the end; God was focused on the means to it. I was searching for direction; God wanted me searching for *Him*. And as I gave myself to Him, in search of direction, He gave Himself to me, preparing me for His direction. Perhaps this explains why God doesn't answer our questions or solve our problems right away. They're really not about the solution; they're about the search for the One who holds the solution.

Early in my fourth month of my sabbatical—He took His sweet time—God made it unmistakably clear that my ministry at Willow Creek Community Church was, in fact, over. I felt completely released. And not only that, but directed to move on.

His obvious leading had come through three primary sources.

First was God's Word—an obvious source, yet often the last place we look. We think, *How can a book written thousands of years ago provide specific guidance for our lives?* Well, it can and it does, because *He* can and *He* does! "For the word of God is living and active" (Heb. 4:12). The Bible isn't merely a history book; it is God's primary means for communicating with us. Any search for direction needs to begin within its pages. He brings His Word to life in order to speak to our current situations. I found this to be the case once again.

A second source of leading came through the counsel of mentors. Over several weeks I spent many hours with a number of spiritual advisers. Together we reviewed who God had made me to be—my spiritual gifts, my passions, my personality, my talents, my experiences. We also discussed my current role at Willow Creek as well as potential future roles, including those with the newly formed Willow Creek Association. After many hours of discussion, one mentor summed up his thoughts in one brief sentence: "There's a better job for you than your current one, and there's a better person for your current job than you."

He was right, and I knew it. For years I'd challenged each Willow Creek employee and volunteer to find an area of ministry that really "turned his crank." Yet nothing was really turning *my* crank. Passion is important in whatever we choose to do with our lives and is essential in ministry. The church of Jesus Christ ought to be the most passion-filled organization on the face of the earth. I'd lost my passion. I hadn't entered the ministry to manage human activity, but that's what I was doing. I needed a change.

The third source of God's unmistakable leading was the Holy Spirit, who shaped—or *re*shaped—the desires of my heart during times of prayer. David tells us, "Delight yourself in the LORD; and He will give you the desires of your heart" (Ps. 37:4). I *had* delighted myself in the Lord. Now my desire (His desire in me, I believe) was to move on.

This was a dramatic shift, and difficult to admit. I'd been a part of the Willow Creek family for more than twenty years, dating back to my involvement in the high school ministry from which the church evolved. I'd envisioned myself at Willow Creek for life. But the simple truth now was that I didn't want to be there anymore. The time had come for me to leave "home."

God had aligned three sources—His Word, godly counsel, and the reshaping of my desires by the Spirit—to redirect my path. Now the question was, To what?

Sometimes God shows us what's next before leading us to the end of *what is*. This is the path of sight, because we can *see* the road ahead. This path is much easier to travel than its counterpart, the path of faith. I'd pressed God hard for *what's next?* but heard no answer. Now I found myself on the path of faith—or should I say, the *limb* of faith. The limb of faith is not an easy place to be, but it's where God resides, for "without faith it is impossible to please Him" (Heb. 11:6).

At times God invites us to step out onto this limb; at other times He pushes us out. I felt shoved! Since God had made it clear I wasn't to return to Willow Creek, moving on was my only choice. But I didn't have any specific job offers to which I felt called.

My wife was out on the limb with me. It's one thing to find yourself on the limb of faith because of your own choices, but it's another to be there because of someone else's choice. Poor MaryAnn. Had it been just the two of us—no problem! We would have been off on an adventure. But three young children have a way of redefining "R & R" to mean "reality and responsibility."

I immediately called five of my spiritual brothers and asked them if they would sacrifice a day to meet with me and help me discern God's leading. They all agreed. I'll always be indebted to these five men who made a sacrifice to walk with a brother. Every pastor should be so fortunate to have men such as these around him.

At the start of our day together, I shared my thoughts on future possibilities:

"I sense no leading to leave vocational ministry and head into the marketplace, but I'm open to it if you see wisdom in that.

"While I can see myself taking a senior pastor position in the future, I don't see myself doing that now. And I don't believe there's wisdom in my taking an executive pastor position in another church at this time.

"I see the value of parachurch ministry, but my heart beats for the church.

"I haven't won the lottery (having not even played it), nor do I have a big inheritance coming my way, therefore I do need a job.

"So ... what do you think I should do?"

My brothers chuckled and made a few sarcastic remarks about "all" the options that existed. We prayed and asked God to make additional options known. By the end of the day, we sensed that God had imparted His wisdom to us. In spite of our not seeing *any* options at first, God made one clear.

One of these brothers said, "God has taken you on a unique journey at Willow Creek. He's given you an incredible breadth of experience." He reminded me how I'd been involved in almost every dimension of the church—children, youth, singles, small groups, worship planning, missions, administration, teaching, staff development, evangelism, and many more. My participation had given me a unique perspective as the church grew from tens to thousands. I was there as the church made the journey from rented facilities to a couple hundred thousand square feet of buildings on more than a hundred acres.

"You've had a unique range of ministry experiences that qualify you to speak into situations like few people can," these brothers told me. Now, with great affirmation, they said they believed God had allowed me to travel this road for a purpose, and that He could now use my years of experience to help others in the same trenches.

Since then, for more than fifteen years, I've had the privilege of coming alongside many in the trenches of ministry, from volunteers to senior leaders of churches and parachurch ministries, with an offer of assistance.

My Second Question

Earlier I mentioned having two key questions that weighed heavily on me during my sabbatical. I've described how God answered my first question—"What is it, God, that You want me to do?"—and I've since experienced the fruit of that answer.

But the second question couldn't be answered so quickly, and in fact is still being answered today: *What's broken, and what will fix it?*

I was broken, and I knew it. I could see the consequences of my brokenness. As I said, I was weary, on edge, mentally drained, and spiritually empty. The ministry is often a place of challenge and trial, and the Bible is clear that we're engaged in a spiritual battle. Paul writes of this challenge in his final exhortation to Timothy:

> Preach the word; be ready in season and out of season; reprove, rebuke, exhort, with great patience and instruction. For the time will come when they will not endure sound doctrine; but wanting to have their ears tickled, they will accumulate for themselves teachers in accordance to their own desires, and will turn away their ears from the truth and will turn aside to myths. But you, be sober in all things, endure hardship, do the work of an evangelist, fulfill your ministry. (2 Tim. 4:2–5)

So life in the trenches of ministry is not a life of ease.

Yet I was sure God had something different in mind for His servants than the pain I was feeling. I didn't know the cause behind my broken condition. I was trying to do all the right things: setting boundaries, monitoring my mental and emotional gauges, and applying the principles of self-care. I also exercised regularly and ate a well-balanced diet (except for ice cream). And again, by all external indicators I was experiencing ministry success. Didn't the numbers prove God was "in it"? *Well, if He's in it, I* wondered, *then why am I in this condition?* In my heart of hearts, I was crying out:

> *God, I want more of You than I'm getting.*
>
> *I'm tired of driving myself to be successful on the playing field of ministry.*
>
> *If this is the price of success, I don't think I can afford it.*
>
> *I'm weary of trying to motivate people to do Your work.*
>
> *God, I need more power.*
>
> *Too much is being done in the flesh, God. I want to be engaged in a move of Your Spirit.*
>
> *If Your yoke is easy, then what's this I'm yoked to?*
>
> *If Your burden is light, whose burden am I carrying?*

Discovering God's response to these cries would take longer than four months. And fixing what was broken would take longer still.

The truth is I had embraced a few heretical beliefs that put me in a sort of bondage. My condition was a consequence of some heretical thinking. I'd spent almost twenty years focused on what God could do *through* me. Addressing my broken condition would require the focus to change—from *through* me to *in* me. What I needed was a paradigm shift, a leadershift. Not an

THE HIGH PRICE OF HERESY

organizational shift, but something personal, a transformation of heart and mind.

I wasn't accustomed to this sort of change. I discovered that transforming the heart and mind is far more difficult than transforming an organization.

Sinking Fast

While churches and ministries certainly need paradigm shifts, the reform most needed is not of the organizational variety, but the individual. Hearts and minds are broken ... and in desperate need of being repaired. Just look at the stats:

> Recently compiled statistics indicate that the life of a pastor is tough. Every month, 1,300 U.S. pastors are fired or forced to resign. Nearly 30 percent of ministers have been terminated at least once. In a decade, 40 percent of today's pastors will be in another line of work. Seventy percent say they have no close friends. The numbers don't improve at home: The divorce rate for U.S. pastors is up at least 65 percent in 25 years. More than one third admit to "inappropriate sexual behavior" with church members. Eighty percent say their work has a negative impact at home.

That's from an October 1996 article in the *Atlanta Journal-Constitution* titled "The Pastorate, Troubled Lives." Its accuracy is confirmed by the following findings from George Barna's organization:

- Two-thirds of the pastors surveyed said they're disturbed because they feel their job is never done.

- Nine out of ten pastors admit that they often take home with them the mental and emotional baggage associated with ministry.

- Eight out of ten pastors confessed that the stress of long workweeks affects them physically. Fifty percent said they suffer physically from stress at least once a month.

- One out of eight pastors is divorced. The divorce rate for U.S. pastors rose 65 percent in the past twenty-five years. Eighty percent of pastors in one survey group said that their ministry has "a negative impact" on their home life, while one-third said the pastorate has been a "hazard" to their families.

- The typical spouse complains more than once per month about the pastor's schedule. One of every two pastors acknowledges that the pastoral workload causes conflict with his or her spouse.

- Seventy-five percent of spouses say they're truly anxious about their finances; two-thirds of pastors feel at least some anxiety about their financial future.

- A seasoned pastoral leader revealed that preachers' kids have an unusually high rate of church disaffection. The evenings-and-weekends nature of church life can make ministers seem like absentee parents who don't have time or energy to be involved with their children or to provide oversight.

Another disturbing picture comes from a Christian Broadcasting Network fact sheet article titled "Pastor Burnout: Combating a Churchwide Epidemic":

> What might be called a spiritual virus is stalking the homes and pulpits of America's pastors. Each year, thousands of clergy walk away from their ministries, suffering from burnout brought on by frantic schedules and unrealistic expectations.... The clergy is like the *Titanic*—it is sinking fast. Fifteen hundred ministers every month drop out of the ministry. That's an epidemic. Even more sobering is that nearly 6,000 Southern Baptist ministers annually fall victim to burnout, depression, marital problems, and even suicide.

A Needed Overhaul

Something is definitely wrong, and not just with those in professional ministry. Laypeople, too, are struggling. They need more of God than they're getting. With jobs of their own and families to raise, the average layperson serving in ministry is already full to the brim with the responsibilities of life.

No matter where I travel, I hear the same complaint: "I'm too busy." One pastor recently told me, "It's easier for me to ask my people to give their money than their time. *Write a check?* No problem. *Give up an evening?* Is that really necessary?" And from all the consulting I've done, I can say with conviction that the average layperson has little interest in expending himself or herself in simply propping up an institution we call the church. There's an intense hunger among laity to be engaged in a movement of God, and these people want God to use *them* to help propel such a movement. The days of "hire the pastor to do the work of the ministry" are fading away—thankfully! Laypeople want to do more than hand out bulletins, count the offering, and attend monthly committee meetings to plan programs and coordinate events.

Unfortunately for many the work of the ministry has become a have-to, should-do responsibility instead of the can't-afford-to-miss-it opportunity that Kingdom work should be. Ministry burnout isn't limited to the clergy. The laity, too, are broken and in search of something more.

The good news: God is in the business of healing broken people. The bad news: Participation in God's work is *producing* broken people. How ironic. We can only conclude that we're not doing God's work God's *way*—and the reason is that heresy has made its way into our thinking.

We need an overhaul. And yes, we need it in our organizations. But that can occur only when the hearts and minds of those within the organization are individually transformed—a *personal* leadershift. When this happens, our values, priorities, and even the way we do church business will change, enabling us to experience the dynamic energy Paul speaks of: "For this purpose also I labor, striving according to His power, which mightily works within me" (Col. 1:29). Paul was well acquainted with God's power. How else could he have accomplished all that he did, while enduring all that he suffered? He did it by the power of God—and this same power is available today, if we'll submit to change.

God has a great deal to say about how the work of His King-dom should be organized and carried out. But today some of our most basic understandings concerning Kingdom work are bro-ken. Our thinking concerning the work of the ministry is, to some degree, in error—heretical, in fact. We've bought into some lies along the way. We're clearly making some mistakes in our practices, and they carry a heavy price—as the statistics indicate.

While it sounds harsh and condemning to say heresy has made its way into the church, it's true. And the cost has been painfully high. Nowhere has that pain been felt more than among leaders.

We must correct the errors in our thinking. We must reject the lies, embrace the truth, and alter our practices. We must align *ourselves* with God's truth ... then align our organizations with God's truth.

Summary

The statistics don't lie. In fact they're sending a strong message that many of us have lost our way. Our thinking, the beliefs that come from it, and the resulting practices we display are taking many lead-ers down a road of self-destruction.

For most this is happening in spite of the best of intentions and the purest of motives. Many don't know any other way and are sim-ply following what they've been taught to believe and do.

We need a leadershift, and in order to experience it, we need to call a time-out and reconsider some of our basic assumptions and beliefs about the work of ministry. This is true for those in voca-tional ministry as well as those who are classified as laity.

These basic assumptions and beliefs include an understanding of why God has called us to participate in the work of His Kingdom. Does God need my help? If not, why does He ask me—even command me—to participate? Our answers to such questions have a great deal to do with why we drive ourselves as we do.

And what constitutes success in ministry? Are we supposed to be successful? How is such success measured? This is where we'll look next ... for the path we take is determined by the destination we seek.

3

THE SUCCESS HERESY

"How do you know whether you're being successful?"

That was the question I recently posed to a small group of pastors. The silence that followed indicated that perhaps they didn't understand what I was asking, so I rephrased it: "How do you measure the success of your ministry?"

More silence. Either they were afraid to say what they thought, or they had no definitive answer.

Finally one pastor responded: "When I walk away feeling good about what just occurred."

"Fruit," replied another. "I look at the fruit."

A third, perhaps answering for everyone else, shrugged and said, "I don't know."

I then asked, "Is being successful important to you? Where would you rate its importance, on a scale of one to ten?"

"Ten," came an immediate reply. All the others nodded in agreement; success was extremely important to them.

Pursuing success *is* important—very important. We all want to be successful. No one gets up in the morning planning to be a failure. No one launches a career with the goal of crashing it, or starts a business intending to go belly-up. No athlete enters the playing field hoping to lose. We're wired with a desire to succeed, whether it's a relationship, the classroom, the marketplace, the athletic field, or the ministry. We resonate with Paul's word: "Do you not know that those who run in a race all run, but only one receives the prize? *Run in such a way that you may win*" (1 Cor. 9:24).

Because success is so important to us, we should have a way to measure it. In the marketplace it's the proverbial bottom line. In the classroom it's the grade. On the field it's wins and losses. In the world measuring success is easy: Look at your numbers. This way of thinking has infiltrated the Kingdom of God. Numbers have become the primary means of measuring ministry success as well.

When I first began consulting, a seasoned ministry veteran said to me, "Don, if you can just help pastors accomplish two things, you'll have more work than you can handle." My curiosity piqued, I asked what those two things were. He answered, "Help them increase their attendance and their budget." He was being coy, but he was also stating the truth. If I could somehow help pastors increase their churches' attendance and financial standings, my services would be in demand. That's because a successful ministry is one that's having an impact in people's lives—and the easiest and most frequent way of measuring that impact is by counting nickels and noses. Of course that's not the only measure of success, but clearly the measure that speaks loudest.

Take, for example, a brochure I received promoting "a conference for pastors and Christian leaders like you who are weary of the noise and long to return to their calling." It showed the photos of the plenary session speakers, along with each one's bio:

Speaker #1: "From a start of 18 people 14 years ago, [church name] has grown to over 6,000 each weekend, with several thousand more in commissioned church plants. [Pastor's name] is known for his bold proclamation of Scripture. His national teaching ministry, [name of ministry], is heard daily on more than 550 stations."

Speaker #2: "From a small handful of members to a congregation of nearly 10,000, the ministry of [church name] continues to grow under the leadership of [pastor's name]. He has been used of the Lord to preach the gospel in [city name] and to see new churches grow out of their congregation to various parts of the city and other parts of the world."

Speaker #3: "As the seventh president of [ministry name], he oversees the entire scope of [ministry name]_education, broadcasting, publishing, and church/conference ministries. A frequent speaker at [national event], he also hosts two radio programs: [name of program] heard daily, and [program name], a weekly international program. He has authored ten books, including ..."

Speaker #4: "He has ministered in churches and conferences throughout the United States as well as in Canada, Central and South America, and Europe. He has published over 150 books, including the popular [name of series] of commentaries on every book of the Bible."

Like most conference flyers, this brochure speaks the language of success we all understand. It tells us, "These speakers are worth hearing because they're *successful.* Just look at their *numbers!*"

Perhaps this explains why large ministries are almost always the ones hosting ministry conferences. They have something to teach the rest of us. After all, their numbers tell us: They're successful!

While numbers do say something, and we would be foolish to disregard them completely, we've set them up as *the* benchmark by which we measure ministry success. Outside of figures we struggle to know how to judge the worth of our work.

The Dangers

In my work with ministry leaders, I've noticed a sort of numbers continuum. The continuum begins with "notice the numbers" and ends with "focused on numbers." While being aware of numbers is valuable, focusing on them will bring dangers like these:

■ *Pride.* "Knowledge makes arrogant," Paul states in 1 Corinthians 8:1. While that's true especially in academic circles, "Numbers make arrogant" is perhaps more true in ministry circles. The pecking order of ministry runs largest to smallest, and those on top are tempted to think more highly of themselves than they ought.

While on staff at Willow Creek, I had many opportunities to sit with other pastors in various conferences. When the invitation came to "tell us about your ministry," this "telling" inevitably involved numbers: of attendees, of staff, of ministries, and more. I'm ashamed to admit that, because of Willow's numbers, I took far too much delight in my own telling. I know firsthand what being puffed up with pride feels like. It's haughty, self-serving, and about as far as one can get from the humility God desires to see in us. When numbers serve as a primary means for measuring success, increasing numbers can produce increasing pride.

■ *Discouragement.* While rising numbers tempt us with pride, falling numbers often bring discouragement.

Gary called me, wanting my help in figuring out why his church was no longer growing (numerically). He'd come on as senior pastor on the heels of a church split, and after a time of healing, the church began to expand. I could hear the delight in his voice as he recalled those glory days: They'd started out at seventy-five, grew to almost 250 over two years, leveled off for a while, then in the next four years grew to almost five hundred.

"But now we're stuck," Gary said, "and we can't seem to get unstuck. We've tried everything." His confusion and discouragement were obvious as he added, "I wonder if I'm the problem. Perhaps the church has outgrown my ability to lead it. Maybe I'm better suited to pastor a smaller church."

Such discouragement is not unique to smaller ministries. Peter is the pastor of a church whose Sunday attendance exceeds three thousand. A level it's been at for four years, following twenty years marked by consistent numeric growth. On several occasions Peter has said to me, "I know I shouldn't be focused on the numbers, but they're hard to ignore. I'm really battling discouragement."

Both these pastors are good and godly men whom God has used, and is using, to have a positive impact in their churches. But both are disheartened because the numbers aren't what they want them to be.

The more we focus on numbers, the more susceptible we are to being either puffed up with pride or beaten down with discouragement. A very fine line separates one condition from the other.

■ *Frustration.* As I became involved with Gary's and Peter's churches, I could clearly see God's activity in both of them. The numbers may have said, "We're stuck," but the Holy Spirit's movement didn't. Lives were being impacted, and the hand of God was evident in the fruit the church produced. Both Gary and Peter readily acknowledged that God was at work; He just wasn't at work to the degree they wanted. They weren't blaming God or anyone else; they were just frustrated, and their frustration was palpable. Their respective staffs could feel it. Rejoicing over what God *was* doing was being smothered by grumbling about what He *wasn't* doing.

In a recent conversation with Peter, we discussed what he called his employees' "morale problem." His frustration—and their "morale problem"—could be attributed to one fact: stagnant numbers. This in spite of the fact that God was at work in their midst.

While morale problems can have a variety of causes, near the top of the list is a leader's heart marked by frustration and discontent. If not addressed, it can lead to the danger of drivenness.

■ *Drivenness.* Do more, work harder, work smarter—get more out of yourself and those around you. We end up pushing ourselves and others to do more than is realistic or healthy.

Jerry is driven. He wants to build a great church. He seems to have an endless list of ideas and boundless energy. He already leads three weekend services (one on Saturday evening, two on Sunday morning) and now he wants to add a fourth. Yet only one of the current services is nearing capacity.

Behind the scenes the ministry team is weary because Jerry's pace is overwhelming. The worship leader told me, "Something has to change. I can't keep doing this. I'm dragging my feet on the idea of adding a fourth service, and I don't think Jerry is very happy with me." Another key player just resigned, while another is secretly interviewing for a position at a church across town.

A culture of drivenness requires the horsepower of driven people in order to keep everything going. But driven people eventually hit a wall. I could take you to more than a few ministries where staff turnover is high and the trail of broken relationships is long. People are seen as expendable, relationships are disposable—and it's all justified by the words *we're growing*. Of course that means *numerically* growing. But experience tells me that higher numbers often mask the brokenness that exists within a driven ministry culture. When the numerical growth stops, this brokenness begins to surface. Issues like staff turnover and declining morale become too obvious to ignore. People on all levels of involvement begin to complain about the pace of life and the toll it's taking on them and their families.

■ *Compromise.* Logic tells us that increased appeal means increased numbers. So we're tempted to compromise our message in order to "up" the appeal.

Rick had been the pastor of an established and more traditional church for more than ten years. He left it because of a desire to see more conversions than he believed the church was geared to produce. Now a church planter, he asked me to watch a videotape of his Sunday service and provide some feedback. After doing so, I didn't know if I had watched a church service or a self-help seminar. A five-minute introduction of the morning's topic came before a secular song, then a drama, then another secular tune, and finally the "sermon." Brief, vague references to a couple of Bible verses provided the spiritual content. The program was well done, entertaining, and provided helpful and inspirational thoughts. Rick really does have a desire to reach the lost. But in attempting to reach them, *he* got lost.

Compromising the message in order to increase its charm and, in turn, the numbers is a very real temptation. Paul warned Timothy about this:

> For the time will come when they will not endure sound doctrine; but wanting to have their ears tickled, they will accumulate for themselves teachers in accordance to their own desires; and will turn away their ears from the truth and will turn aside to myths. But you, be sober in all things, endure hardship, do the work of an evangelist, fulfill your ministry. (2 Tim. 4:3–5)

Paul doesn't reveal the "hardship" Timothy was encouraged to endure; perhaps some of it was caused by stagnant or declining numbers, since Paul said that many would "turn away" and "turn aside." That's numerical loss to be sure. Still, he was not to water down the message.

If Jesus had focused on numbers, He would have chased the rich young ruler and said, "I'm sorry. I didn't mean *literally* 'sell everything.' It's just a figure of speech." And He would have softened the hard things He said that caused some of His disciples to stop following Him (John 6:60–66).

When numbers define success, we're inclined to appeal to as many as possible. Sermons about God's love tend to far outnumber sermons about God's holiness. We may altogether abandon sermons on hardship, persecution, and suffering.

■ *Comparison.* Human beings are prone to compare. It's just natural (for the flesh, that is) to compare ourselves with others. This comparison always contains judgment; we can't compare without rendering a judgment. And when numbers are the primary measure of success, it's only natural for me to compare my numbers to your numbers, then judge myself as more or less successful.

The ugliness of such thinking doesn't stop there. I'm also now tempted to compete with you. Just as businesses compete for customers and athletes compete for trophies, ministries compete for numbers. Who's the biggest? The wealthiest? Who owns the most land? Best and biggest buildings? Largest staff? Most ministries? The numbers tell us where we place in the contest. Some are more successful, others less.

The more we move from being merely aware of numbers to being focused on them, the more inclined we are to comparison, to the judgment it contains, and to the competition it produces. I've had ministry leaders confess to resentment and jealousy toward those who are experiencing greater degrees of "success." These attitudes reveal what I call a "kingdom (little 'k') mentality," instead of a "Kingdom mentality." Comparison and competition pit my "kingdom" against your "kingdom," though we both claim to be about *the* Kingdom.

■ *Spiritual Presumption.* It's dangerous to conclude, based on numbers, that God is or isn't "blessing" our efforts. With a focus on numbers comes the temptation to presume we know the degree to which His blessing is given—the greater the numbers, the greater the proof that He's at work. Conversely, when the numbers go down, we think God's activity is slowing.

How many times have you heard someone say, "God is really blessing," then point to growing numbers as evidence? This is a hazardous assumption. If this were true, then many cults and false religions claiming to be of God must, in fact, be right about that, given their growing numbers. On the other hand we would have judged Jesus' ministry on earth to be a failure, since He left a scant 120 in an upper room after He ascended into heaven. Numbers alone can hardly reveal the fruitfulness of a ministry.

Apart from a couple of phrases early in Acts (2:41; 4:4) about the believers in Jerusalem, the New Testament makes no mention of specific numbers in the churches. We don't know how many people made up the church at Corinth, or Ephesus, or Philippi, or any other church for that matter. Paul didn't notice, didn't care, didn't know, or just didn't consider it important enough to mention. But had the New Testament been written in our current ministry culture, each epistle would have begun with membership statistics for the church being stated, followed by an explanation for why the church was or wasn't growing numerically, along with a step-by-step plan to increase attendance.

Yet the few New Testament references that indicate numerical increase (like Acts 2:47—"And the Lord was adding to their number day by day those who were being saved") point to the fact that such growth was God's doing. "I planted," Paul writes, "Apollos watered, but *God was causing the growth*" (1 Cor. 3:6). Whether we interpret such "growth" as spiritual, statistical, or both, the bottom line is that God caused it! How much growth did He bring about? The passage doesn't say. Evidently He didn't feel it was important for us to know.

How God Measures Success

Defining success with numbers is harmful because it appeals more to the flesh than to the Spirit. It takes more life than it gives, fueling pride in some, while bringing discouragement to others.

If we're going to focus on figures, perhaps we should notice exactly how many leaders are battling despair these days due to discouraging numbers. That alone ought to tell us something's wrong.

We need a new target—and a new yardstick, one that measures according to the Spirit, not the flesh. God, not man, is responsible for the scope of one's ministry. While we can certainly celebrate increasing numbers, our reasons for celebration should be greater and deeper than numbers alone. If we remember that God's Kingdom, not our kingdom, is what matters, then we should be filled with joy wherever we see the Kingdom increasing. Success must be seen through God's eyes and measured using God's grid.

So the real question is this: How can you know if your ministry is a success *in God's eyes?* Listen again to Paul:

> But to me it is a very small thing that I may be examined by you, or by any human court; in fact, I do not even examine myself. For I am conscious of nothing against myself, yet I am not by this acquitted; but the one who examines me is the Lord. Therefore do not go on passing judgment before the time, but wait until the Lord comes who will both bring to light the things hidden in the darkness and disclose the motives of men's hearts; and then each man's praise will come to him from God. (1 Cor. 4:3–5)

God is the one to whom we'll answer; He will dispense whatever praise we receive. So how does *He* measure success? That's all that matters! And the Bible provides some answers.

I'd like you to consider four questions. They're biblical questions intended for every believer—not just those in vocational ministry—because God wants us all to pursue success as He defines it. These questions should be answered in terms of your life in general, not merely in terms of church or ministry involvement.

Question 1: Are You Being Faithful?

I, like you, long to hear God say, "Well done, good and faithful servant." Hearing those words would shout success.

Jesus' parable about the "talents" is the context for that familiar phrase:

> For it is just like a man about to go on a journey, who called his own slaves and entrusted his possessions to them. To one he gave five talents, to another, two, and to another, one, each according to his own ability; and he went on his journey. (Matt. 25:14–15)

Note that the *owner* distributed the talents, and he did so according to each slave's ability. It's a biblical fact that God gifts us differently, and to differing degrees. Based on this alone, we should realize that the results of our respective ministries will also differ, as the parable bears out. Recall what happens to the first two slaves:

THE SUCCESS HERESY 71

Immediately the one who had received the five talents went and traded with them, and gained five more talents. In the same manner the one who had received the two talents gained two more....

Now after a long time the master of those slaves came and settled accounts with them. The one who had received the five talents came up and brought five more talents, saying, "Master, you entrusted five talents to me. See, I have gained five more talents." His master said to him, "Well done, good and faithful slave. You were faithful with a few things, I will put you in charge of many things; enter into the joy of your master."

Also the one who had received the two talents came up and said, "Master, you entrusted two talents to me. See, I have gained two more talents." His master said to him, "Well done, good and faithful slave. You were faithful with a few things, I will put you in charge of many things; enter into the joy of your master." (25:16–23)

It is extremely important to note that both of these slaves received the exact same commendation This fact shows us the stark contrast between the economy of God's Kingdom, where success is based not on numbers but on faithfulness—and the economy of the world. In the world the one who produced five more talents would have received a far greater commendation than the one who produced only two more. In this way we adopt the ways of this world whenever we give greater commendation to those with greater numbers.

You'll also remember from the parable that the slave given only one talent "went away, and dug a hole in the ground and hid his master's money" (25:18)—and was found to be unfaithful. He failed! As a result the master rebuked and punished him, and took the talent from him and gave it to another (25:26–28). This response from the master wasn't based on a numerical standard; the master simply wanted to know, "What did you do with what *I* gave *you*?"

This is the first dimension of faithfulness: What has God given you? Do you *know* what you've been given? The answer to this important question certainly includes your natural talents, material resources, and educational training.

It definitely includes spiritual gifts as well, about which Paul writes, "Now concerning spiritual gifts, brethren, I do not want you to be unaware" (1 Cor. 12:1). While we can afford to be ignorant about some areas of life, spiritual gifts isn't one of them. Paul adds, "But to each one is given the manifestation of the Spirit for the common good.... But one and the same Spirit works all these things, distributing to each one individually just as He wills" (12:7, 11). You have a spiritual gift, at least one—probably more. Do you know your gifts? Are you using them? This is central to being faithful.

Many believers are unaware of their gifting. I'm amazed at the number of ministry leaders, pastors included, who have little idea what their spiritual gifts are. If that's you, do something to change it. Many books on spiritual gifts are available, as well as spiritual gift assessments that can point you in the right direction. Seminars, such as *Network*, are designed to help you discover your gifts. Or go to your ministry leader and ask him or her to help you. Your spiritual gifts are the place of God's power in your service for Him. Discover what they are.

Then make a list of what else you've been given: natural talents, material assets, educational training, relationships, passions, and anything else. God can and will use all that He has given you for His glory and your blessing. Your ability to be faithful starts with knowing what God has given you.

Once you identify what God has given you, it's time to invest it in order to contribute to the Kingdom. Do you know what you've been called to contribute? That's the second dimension of faithfulness. Are you called to teach God's Word? To shepherd a small group of younger believers? To dispense mercy to those who are hurting? Are you called to give generously of your resources to support the work? To feed the hungry? To share the gospel with the lost? To extend hospitality to the homeless? Are you called to a ministry of intercessory prayer?

None of us can make a focused and significant contribution to all the ministries that exist. This is why God gives us different gifts, passions, and callings.

To what place of ministry has He called you? For each of us, this calling will pour forth from what God has given us, and whatever that is, we're to use it to serve others "as good stewards of the manifold grace of God" (1 Peter 4:10). *To hear the words "Well done, good and faithful servant," you must do what God has called you to do, using that which He has given you.* In God's eyes this is where success in life and ministry begins.

Question 2: Are You Bearing Fruit?

Jesus said, "My Father is glorified by this, that you bear much fruit, and so prove to be My disciples" (John 15:8). He also told us that God prunes every fruit-bearing branch "that it may bear more fruit" (15:2). God is into fruit. He wants you to bear fruit. For many years I understood this to mean "accomplishing things for God." So I worked hard to accomplish what I thought was on God's to-do list; the more I finished from that list, the more fruit I bore. I now know my understanding was not only incomplete but off target.

Let me explain by going back to my four-month break in the summer of 1992, when I prayed fervently for God to tell me what He wanted me to do. For three months I asked this. I asked Him to show me what He wanted me to accomplish next—but I wasn't getting any reply.

One day the silence broke. I can still remember the time and place when I heard the voice of the Holy Spirit within: *I am not nearly as concerned with what you* do *as I am with who you* are. *And who you are is failing.* I didn't hear an audible voice, but I may as well have, because the Holy Spirit was that clear. The words didn't come as a condemnation but as words of mercy.

Immediately I grabbed my Bible, feeling prompted to turn to Galatians 5:22–23: "But the fruit of the Spirit is love, joy, peace, patience, kindness, goodness, faithfulness, gentleness, self-control; against such things there is no law." I began to evaluate myself in light of those nine characteristics.

Love. How was I doing as a lover of others? The answer wasn't good, so I jumped quickly to the next trait.

Joy. Oh, no, this was getting worse. *Better move on*, I thought.

Peace. Wow! I was one of the most stressed-out people I knew.

Patience. Not exactly my strong suit. In fact any line requiring me to stand behind someone else was too long for me. I hated waiting.

As I continued down the list, my spirits sank lower. It wasn't until I came to *faithfulness* that I had any reason to feel good about myself. I *was* faithful; I knew that. But as my chest began to fill with pride over that fact, I moved on to *gentleness*—and I bottomed out. Gentle Don I was not. Fortunately I ended on a higher note with *self-control.*

I sat back in my chair to review my score, *Well*, I thought, *I'm two for nine.* I'd played a lot of baseball growing up, and I understood that stat. It was an unacceptable average for someone who had been a Christian as long as I had. And on top of it, I was supposed to be a *leader*!

The convicting truth was that I was failing to bear fruit. I further realized that even the good marks I could give myself in faithfulness and self-control were due mostly to my God-given temperament and family background—while seven other "fruits" were found lacking.

For three months I'd asked God what He wanted me to do; now He was saying, "Wrong question. You've spent twenty years focused on 'doing,' and it's left you exhausted and empty. You've depended more on fleshly faithfulness and self-control than you have on Me. But you mean more to Me than all your 'doing' does. It's time to shift your focus—to move to a new place in Me, in order to bear more fruit."

Suddenly I knew: I was about to get pruned.

The world's system doesn't measure success based on the fruit of the Spirit. Love, joy, peace, gentleness—those can't be measured with numbers. Scoring goodness or assigning a grade to kindness is tough. Yet this is what God measures. They may not win awards on earth, but they do in heaven.

Are you bearing the fruit of the Holy Spirit's influence? I would encourage you to look at yourself through the lens of the nine characteristics of the fruit of the Spirit. The world may not measure success based on character traits, but God does. Loving others, experiencing and expressing joy, reflecting and spreading peace—all are ingredients of success in God's eyes.

You can probably identify two or three of these characteristics that come naturally to you. What about the others that require the work of the Spirit? Are you succeeding?

While the fruit of the Spirit is one measure of fruitfulness, the New Testament speaks of a second kind of fruitfulness. This is the fruitfulness of Christlike influence. While the fruit of the Holy Spirit is internal, the fruit of Jesus' influence is external. Peter spoke of this influence in Acts 10:38: "You know of Jesus of Nazareth, how God anointed Him with the Holy Spirit and with power, and how He went about doing good and healing all who were oppressed by the devil, for God was with Him." Jesus went about *doing good*—it happened naturally as He traveled through life. "Doing good" wasn't in His job description; it was in *Him*. As He lived day by day, His goodness came out and touched others, whether through teaching, healing, clothing, or feeding.

The same should be said of you and me. The more of Christ we have within, the more naturally His goodness will come forth in our daily lives. What "good" are you currently engaged in doing?

What "good" came forth from your life today? How did others benefit as you traveled in your world this week? To have the influence
of Jesus is to do good for those who cross your path.

In Peter's description of Jesus, he mentions the ultimate good:
"healing all who were oppressed by the devil." Jesus worked to take
back from the devil that which rightfully belongs to God.

This reminds us that people are at the top of the list, and Jesus
worked to set people free. Whether their bondage was spiritual,
emotional, mental, physical, or relational, Jesus released them.

Through us the fruit of His influence brings freedom to those
around us who are oppressed. Are you engaged in a work to set people free? What specific influence is Jesus having in the world
through your life? Who's being released? In what ways are they
being influenced?

These are the questions we need to consider in any attempt to
measure success God's way. Look for the fruit, both internal and
external. I would encourage you to take a few minutes right now to
consider the answer to these important questions.

As for the number of lives that are touched—that's God's job.
As Albert Einstein once said, "Not all that counts can be counted,
and not all that can be counted counts." Let God handle the
numbers.

Question 3: Are You Fulfilled?

My dictionary defines *fulfill* as, among other things, "to make full."
Is your life, is your ministry, making you full?

Full of *what*? you ask.

Joy. Remember the master's invitation to the two "good and faithful" slaves? *"Enter into the joy of your master."* Joy is one of the primary blessings of faithful and fruitful service.

This is exactly what Jesus indicated as He concluded His remarks in John 15 about fruit-bearing: "These things I have spoken to you so that My joy may be in you, and *that your joy may be made full"* (15:11). Jesus taught them to bear fruit so they would know His joy and experience it in the fullest way.

One who bears fruit should receive the blessing of joy. In the Gospels this is seen clearly in the experience of those whom Jesus sent out in ministry: "The seventy returned with *joy,* saying, 'Lord, even the demons are subject to us in Your name'" (Luke 10:17). Of all the words that Luke could have used there to describe their ministry experience, isn't it interesting that he chose the word *joy?*

Such joy is the result of faithful and fruitful living. Are you experiencing this fulfillment? Do you lay your head on your pillow at night with an inner sense of satisfaction, knowing God is influencing the world through your life? Experiencing God's joy in life and ministry is a sign of success. This is a joy only God can give—and He does indeed give it to the faithful and the fruitful.

Question 4: Are You Making God Famous?

This is the bottom line, the ultimate measure of your life and ministry: Is God becoming famous through you?

A friend of mine—I'll call him Dave—began a financial services company in the early '90s. A young believer at the time, Dave took his newfound faith in Christ seriously and grew dramatically in spiritual matters. At the same time, God was blessing his company's efforts; it, too, grew exponentially. By the end of the decade, Dave was earning far more than he needed to support his family. While he and his wife were giving faithfully and generously to their church and other ministries, they began to sense that God was calling them to go beyond their current giving. They decided to start a charitable foundation.

One day Dave called to ask if I would help them put together a giving plan for the foundation, so I met with them. "Why do you want to start a foundation?" I asked at our initial meeting. I assumed I knew the answer, but I wanted to hear it straight from them.

Their answer surprised me. "We want to put the generosity of God on display. Since becoming Christians, we've noticed that many people, Christians included, believe God is stingy. Our experience is just the opposite, and we want to help change that perception. We want others to experience God's generosity."

From the very beginning of our discussion, they made it clear this foundation wasn't about *their* generosity, but God's. They saw themselves as nothing more than pens that God would use to write checks from His checkbook. The implications of this perspective were profound. They didn't name the foundation for themselves; they instead chose a name from Scripture that reflected God's heart toward those in need. They wouldn't personally sign checks going out from the foundation. And with each check would come a cover letter indicating that this was a gift from God, for He was the one who had given the power to make wealth (Deut. 8:18). They made every attempt to divert attention away from them and onto God.

Such a perspective should be at the heart of *all* ministry. Listen to these words:

> Whoever speaks, is to do so as one who is speaking the utterances of God; whoever serves is to do so as one who is serving by the strength which God supplies; *so that in all things God may be glorified through Jesus Christ, to whom belongs the glory and dominion forever and ever.* Amen. (1 Peter 4:11)

When someone speaks God's truth, the listeners' response should be, "Isn't God great? Isn't His truth wonderful?" This is in sharp contrast with the responses heard today, which typically focus on the effectiveness of the communicator.

Service should be rendered with a spirit that points to God's power at work in the servant. In this way we can be compared to agents or publicists hired to represent clients. While we know the name of the celebrity, we seldom know the name of his or her representative, yet it is this person who helps make the celebrity famous.

Success in our ministry is ultimately measured by the degree to which God becomes famous:

> Let your light shine before men in such a way that they may see your good works, and glorify your Father who is in heaven. (Matt. 5:16)

> My Father is glorified by this, that you bear much fruit, and so prove to be My disciples. (John 15:8)

Summary

I don't want to go too far and say numbers shouldn't matter at all, or should never be looked at. Noticing numbers *is* valuable; we can learn some things from them (trends and patterns, for example). Trouble is, we've swung the pendulum way too far in that direction. Danger arises when "noticing" becomes "focusing." A focus on numbers will leave you susceptible to pride or discouragement; it can open the door to unnecessary feelings of frustration or to a drivenness that reflects nothing more than fleshly ambition.

Watching numbers too closely will almost certainly lead you to compare your ministry with that of others. The judgment behind such comparison and the competition it can fuel often serve as sources of division among God's servants. Perhaps worst of all is the temptation to compromise the truth of the gospel in order to increase its appeal.

When we stop to consider the list of dangers associated with a focus on numbers—pride, discouragement, frustration, drivenness, compromise, comparison, judgment, competition, and spiritual presumption—we should be able to discern the presence of heresy. That list has nothing to do with the Kingdom of God. Success defined by numbers is the language of this world, and reflects the economy upon which this world is built. Applying the language and economy of this world to the Kingdom of God is unsafe and unsound.

Success in God's eyes means abiding in faithfulness, in fruitfulness, and in fulfillment (the experience of His joy). And He delights when His name is made famous among the people He created. Therefore strive to be found faithful. Abide in Him so you bear much fruit. Long for the true fulfillment that faithful and fruitful living produces. Labor to make His name famous.

Imagine for a moment what your church or ministry would be like if every believer was successful in *biblical* terms—faithful, fruitful, fulfilled, and engaged in making God famous. Everyone a success! Envision what such a body of believers would look and feel like. Picture the response such a ministry would create in the world around it. While such an objective may not be as quantifiable as other measures, it's worth pursuing ... because it's God's measurement of success.

God is calling you to help His people experience biblical success. And in the end *He* will take care of the numbers.

4

THE SERVING HERESY

When my children were between the ages of three and eight, they seemed to ask a hundred "why" questions a day, all for perfectly good reasons.

"Why is the lake blue?" *It's not blue when I hold the water in my hand.*

"Why do I need to brush my teeth in the morning?" *I brushed them before bed, and they can't get dirty while I'm sleeping.*

"Why do you have to go to work?" *Stay home and play with me.*

"Why do I have to take a bath?" *I just took one last week.*

"Why did God make mosquitoes?" *You told me He was perfect.*

"Why do I always have to finish my vegetables?" *You never make me finish dessert.*

Why, why, *why?*

These questions from kids may seem trivial at times, but our own "why" questions often need answers ASAP. Like when it's

January in Michigan (where I live) and your furnace goes out. Or your car won't start. Or you're experiencing chest pain, shortness of breath, and dizziness.

Some pretty important "why" questions exist in the spiritual realm as well. Jesus addresses a few of them in Matthew 6, when He issues warnings about our works of righteousness. In effect He asks His audience to consider why they give, why they pray, and why they fast. Our motives are very important to God, so they should also be important to us.

We see the same significance in these words from Paul:

> Therefore do not go on passing judgment before the time, but wait until the Lord comes who will both bring to light the things hidden in the darkness and disclose the motives of men's hearts; and then each man's praise will come to him from God. (1 Cor. 4:5)

Why we serve in the Kingdom is a matter of motive, and therefore important for each of us to consider.

Our answer to that will be based on our understanding of another "why" question: Why has God called us to participate in the work of His Kingdom? What is He after?

This is critical, since "serving the Lord" is not an elective for us, but a requirement: "Therefore, my beloved brethren, be steadfast, immovable, *always abounding in the work of the Lord*" (1 Cor. 15:58). Jesus told His followers, "We must work the works of Him who sent me as long as it is day; night is coming when no man one work" (John 9:4). He instructed them not only to participate in this work, but also to pray for the Father to raise up *more* workers:

"The harvest is plentiful, but the laborers are few; therefore beseech the Lord of the harvest to send out laborers into His harvest" (Luke 10:2).

Participation in the work of the Kingdom is God's will for every believer. Any believer who fails to participate is in direct disobedience to God. Further, anyone claiming to be a follower of Jesus, yet doesn't desire to participate in His work, needs to do some soul-searching about the authenticity of his or her faith. Why? Because the heart of every sincere believer longs to see the Father's will done on earth as it is in heaven.

This explains why Paul wrote, "Now concerning spiritual gifts, brethren, I do not want you to be unaware" (1 Cor. 12:1). Ignorance on the topic of spiritual gifts is unacceptable. Their significance—for believers individually, and for the Kingdom of God as a whole—is so great that spiritual gifts must not be overlooked. Knowing your spiritual gift is critical to your ability to participate in Kingdom work as God intends.

But *why* is our participation in this work required? Why is our contribution such a big deal to God? The answer to this question has a profound influence on our motive for serving, in addition to providing insight about why God measures success as He does.

Without fully comprehending the significance of this "why" question, I spent many years actively participating in God's work. The Bible told me this work was God's will, and I wanted to live within His will. My heart, like the heart of every believer, is inclined toward pleasing God. So I assumed that I participated because I wanted to obey and glorify God by accomplishing His purposes.

While that answer explained (from my perspective) why I

serve the Lord, it didn't explain (from God's perspective) why He calls me to serve. God has His reasons—and they're good ones, of course. But before I get to them, let me address a couple of serving-related heresies.

Serving Heresy 1: God Needs Help

Saying God needs our help with *anything* sounds almost blasphemous. But I think most of us, subconsciously at least, believe that He does. Otherwise why would He ask us to participate?

Yesterday I called a friend to see if he could come over and help me cut down a dead tree in the backyard. Why did I call him? Because I needed help. If I hadn't needed help, I wouldn't have asked. We assume God's logic must work the same way.

Verses like this one seem to support that notion:

> How then will they call on Him in whom they have not believed? How will they believe in Him whom they have not heard? And how will they hear without a preacher? (Rom. 10:14)

Isn't Paul saying, "God needs a preacher, or else those who need to hear won't hear"? It sounds as though God needs my help.

But compare that thought to these words:

> The God who made the world and all things in it, since He is Lord of heaven and earth, does not dwell

in temples made with hands; *nor is He served by human hands, as though He needed anything,* since He Himself gives to all people life and breath and all things. (Acts 17:24–25)

While there appears to be a contradiction between these two passages, no contradiction exists. What does exist is a mystery. This mystery boggles our minds, but not God's.

The truth is, He doesn't need our help. God is fully *self*-sufficient and *all*-sufficient. The One who spoke the universe into existence is not dependent on any preacher to bring forth His Word. He's able to do whatever He pleases, whenever He pleases, with whomever He pleases. He isn't sitting on His throne—now or ever—anxiously wringing His hands, hoping you'll be persuaded to join His work lest it fail to get accomplished. The eternal destiny of our unsaved neighbors doesn't sit with us. If it did, the pressure of His work would be crushing.

At the same time—and here's the mystery—God *uses* you and me to bring the gospel to our neighbors. It's through our proclaiming of the gospel that Christ brings salvation.

This is what Paul seeks to convey in that question, "How will they hear without a preacher?" He's simply affirming his own authority, as one sent by God, to proclaim the gospel so others may be saved. God has chosen to link Himself with us in the accomplishment of His eternal purposes. He uses us to make a difference in the world.

We *do* make a critical difference in accomplishing this work. But the key is this: God gives us this opportunity to be difference-makers *for our blessing.*

Continuing that same passage, Paul goes on to say,

> How will they preach unless they are sent? Just as it is
> written, "How beautiful are the feet of those who bring
> good news of good things!" (Rom. 10:15)

God sends us for the joy of being sent. It's not for *His* blessing
that He calls us, *for He is in need of nothing.* Therefore, if we fail to
cooperate with Him in being difference-makers, the loss is ours.
The blessing is then passed on to someone who will obey His call.

God doesn't *need* us, but He does *want* us—out of His great
love for us. He wants you to receive all the blessings that come
through participation with Him in the accomplishment of His purposes. His call for your involvement is based on His love for you,
not His need for help. God's desire is to give you something, not
take something from you.

Serving Heresy 2: God Wants a Payback

It's payback time! We know all about that, don't we? You send me a
birthday gift, so I send you a birthday gift. You invite me over to
dinner; I need to reciprocate. You treated for lunch last time; it's my
treat next time. Payback.

The psalmist wrote, "What shall I render to the LORD for all
His benefits toward me?" (Ps. 116:12). Paraphrased: "How can I
express my thanks for all He has done for me?" For many years one
of my primary responses was, "I'll join His work. I'll work my tail
off to convey my appreciation for everything God has done for

me." Chances are, you, too, have seen your participation in God's work as a way of saying thanks.

But is this what God wants? In a word, *no!* While thankfulness to God is good, payback is not.

First of all, plain and simple, we can't do it.

Second, the concept of payback is self-serving and therefore offensive to God. Let me illustrate.

I have a mortgage on my house. Therefore I have a relationship of sorts with my mortgage company. In all my correspondence with them, they refer to me as a "customer." In fact I write my "customer number" on every check I send in payment of my debt. But truth be told, I'm not a customer; I'm a debtor. Our relationship is based on *my* indebtedness. The company not only expects payback from me; it demands it.

Imagine with me for a moment that the president of the mortgage company called one day with this good news: "Mr. Cousins, we have an annual drawing in which we randomly select one customer whose loan we mark 'paid in full.' This year your name was selected. Therefore your debt is canceled."

If that were to happen, I would no longer have a relationship with them based on debt. Our future relationship would be based on the grace they displayed in forgiving my debt.

In the spiritual realm there was a time when we were "debtors" in relationship to God. But with the payment of Jesus' blood, and our acceptance of it, our debt was erased and marked "paid in full." There's no more payback.

The debt payment required an act of grace, and our relationship with God is now based on that grace. We cannot pay God back for all He has done for us. To try is futile. More importantly any attempt on our part is in effect saying, "Your grace isn't sufficient for me; I have to pay You back." Our works of service would direct credit our way for having merited a relationship with God. And the Bible is clear that *our* works of righteousness are as filthy rags to God. We live and serve dependent upon God's grace—past, present, and future. God isn't looking for a reimbursement. He's a God of grace.

But so what? Why's it so important that we bring truth to these heretical notions?

Here are a couple of good reasons.

First, we need to understand that our participation in God's work has no impact on His love for us. Whether we serve little, much, or none at all has no influence on the degree of His love for us. Having been raised with a strong work ethic and a respectful understanding of "payback," I don't find it easy to comprehend or accept that my "serving" does nothing to merit additional favor from God. But it's true: I already have His favor, for I'm a child of grace. God isn't asking for something in return for all He has done for us. Our relationship with Him is based on His grace alone.

This truth is extremely difficult for all of us to truly grasp, because the economy of our world and relationships are seldom based on grace. Having "favor" with my mortgage company, for example, is completely dependent on my making payments. If I stop making those, I'll very quickly fall into disfavor with them. The same "disfavor" typically comes into play in most of our relationships when we fail to apply the "payback" principle.

While we can understand that we *enter* a relationship with God based on His grace, we seemingly fall prey to believing that our *continued* relationship with Him is based on good works. This is heretical thinking and places the one who believes it in a form of bondage. We "do and do and do for God," thinking that all our "doing" will increase His favor—the more we do, the more of His love and blessings we'll receive. Such "doing" can be downright exhausting, as well as lacking in joy because of the sense of obligation it carries. Moreover, all this "doing" is self-centered—it's service focused on self, not on God.

We need to be delivered from such thinking and the bondage it produces. The truth is, we build an ongoing relationship with God out of the same grace with which we enter that relationship. And the serving we do is dependent on His grace—a truth the apostle Peter points us to: "As each one has received a special gift, employ it in *serving one another as good stewards of the manifold grace of God*" (1 Peter 4:10).

Second, and even more importantly, we need to dismiss these heretical notions about "serving God" because of the impact they have on our concept of who God is. You've probably heard it said that the most important thoughts you'll ever have are those you have about God. Who you see God to be is paramount to the way you relate to Him. Seeing God as One who wants to *get* something from you (your service, your help) is dramatically different from seeing God as One who wants to *give* you something—His grace and blessings.

Do you perceive God as One who's looking to extract something from you for His benefit, or as One who looks to pour something into you for your benefit? As leaders this not only affects how we relate to God in the midst of our service, but it also deeply impacts the way we lead others in their service.

The Truth about Serving

So why *does* God call us to participate in the work of His Kingdom? The answer to this important "why" question comes in two parts.

Biblical Truth 1: Our participation in the work of His Kingdom brings His blessings to and through our lives.

I once heard Warren Wiersbe define blessing as "something God gives to us for our good and His glory." I like that definition, and it certainly fits with these words from Paul: "Blessed be the God and Father of our Lord Jesus Christ, who has *blessed us with every spiritual blessing* in the heavenly places in Christ" (Eph. 1:3). Paul goes on to list some of these blessings that God gives to us for our good and His glory. The implication: *God has called you and me to take part in His work in order to give us something, not take something away.* God is the Giver; we are the receivers. It must always be this way, because givers get the glory.

I first heard John Piper illustrate this important truth using the context of the benefactor/beneficiary relationship. Let me illustrate.

After spending most of my life in the Chicago area, our family moved a few years ago to west Michigan. As I became familiar with the Grand Rapids area in particular, the number of buildings bearing the name of an individual struck me: hospitals, arenas, museums, and others. I learned that these buildings were named after the primary benefactor whose contribution helped make the building possible. In this way the benefactor is honored (receives "glory," if you will) for his or her contribution to the work. While not judging anyone's motive for such a contribution, notice that it's the benefactor, not the beneficiary, who always gets the credit (the glory).

This is true on the spiritual level as well. Therefore God must always be seen as the benefactor. If we, in our serving, take on the role of benefactor and make God the beneficiary, we receive the glory for what's accomplished.

In all our serving we must maintain the role of beneficiary, and God the benefactor. He has called us to participate in His work in order to give us something—His blessings. That's profound! He calls us so He can give, not take. As Jesus said, "Even the Son of Man did not come to be served, but to serve, and to give His life a ransom for many" (Mark 10:45).

God "does" for us. And if we fail to respond to His call, we forfeit the blessings He wants to bestow upon us. And who wants to do that?

While what I've just stated is in accordance with biblical truth, we apparently are not applying it. I make this claim based on personal experience and observation. You'll recall my account in chapter 2 of how I became physically run down, emotionally strung out, mentally fatigued, and spiritually empty. But would that have been my experience if I had correctly embraced God's role as benefactor and mine as beneficiary? What about the thousands and thousands of pastors who are living "troubled lives"? Would that be true if they correctly embraced the nature of our benefactor/beneficiary relationship with God? And would countless believers in the body of Christ be sitting in the stands with regard to the work of the Kingdom if they understood the blessings they're forfeiting as a result? I think not.

While this isn't the only explanation for our troubled condition or the lack of participation among believers, it's certainly one of the causes.

God is a gracious benefactor. He's calling us to the work of His Kingdom in order to bring His blessings to us and through us. These blessings come by grace, out of His great love for us. This explains in part why God has called us to His work. While this alone should stir us to worship, we have more to uncover as we seek to answer the question of why God calls us to His work.

Biblical Truth 2: God displays Himself through His blessings to us, thereby bringing glory to His name.

Let me go back to the friend I mentioned who began a charitable foundation to display God's generosity. He and his wife made the deliberate choice not to name the foundation after themselves. They also opted to have someone else sign the checks. Each check goes out with a cover letter explaining that God is the source of all provision. While they're not obsessed with keeping their identity a secret, they've made every attempt to showcase God's name so He gets the honor for "their" giving. God's generosity is what makes *their* giving possible in the first place, and their ability to bless others is entirely dependent upon Him.

The apostle Peter affirms this truth: "As each one has *received* a special gift ..." Then what? Peter goes on to say we're to "employ it in serving one another as good stewards of the manifold grace of God" (1 Peter 4:10). As servants we're to steward the grace of God. We give based on the grace, or blessing, we receive. *If we fail to receive the blessings that come as a result of the manifold grace of God,* *then our serving has no source of energy from which to draw its power.* Our own energy to serve will eventually run out. The result is life-less, passionless performance at the least, and total burnout at the worst. Our service then either stops altogether or is reduced to an act of duty.

Peter affirms the right progression: "Whoever speaks, is to do so as one who is speaking the utterances of God; whoever serves is to do so as one who is serving by the strength which God supplies" (4:11a). The one who speaks God's truth must first be a recipient of that truth. Once blessed personally by the truth, the speaker is empowered to impart the blessing to others. The one who serves must first be a recipient of the power needed to serve.

In this regard we're like extension cords. Left to ourselves, we have no power. But "plugged in," we're able to extend power where it's needed. Servants must be "plugged in" to the Source in order to distribute real power *"so that in all things God may be glorified* *through Jesus Christ,* to whom belongs the glory and dominion for-ever and ever. Amen" (4:11b).

In the end, God, not the speaker or servant, is seen as the source of both truth and power. As the source, the benefactor, God receives the fame as His attributes are displayed through us.

Another Heresy: Serving Is Doing Something for God

Before I bring this chapter on serving heresy to a close, I need to address one more overarching heresy related to serving.

What does it really mean to "serve the Lord"?

Ask the average believer how he or she is serving the Lord, and you'll probably be told of a specific *ministry* the person is involved in: "I serve the Lord in the youth ministry"; "I serve the Lord in the music ministry"; "I serve the Lord as head of the single-parent ministry." You get the idea. For seventeen years I would have told you I served the Lord as a staff member at Willow Creek Community Church. We seemingly define "serving the Lord" as something we *do* at a specific time and place, an act of service we *perform* for the Lord. But this is a shallow and inaccurate (heretical) understanding of serving Him.

I've already explained that God is always the giver (the benefactor). It must be this way, because givers receive the glory. "Doing something for God" would make *Him* the beneficiary—which is problematic. In truth the serving we do is not for Him, but rather for *one another*. The person serving in the youth ministry is providing a service to the students. One who serves in the music ministry is doing something for those who hear the music. And so on. As a staff pastor my service was for the benefit of the people of the church.

Listen carefully to Peter's words: "As each one has received a special gift, employ it in serving *one another*." So the spiritual gifts God distributes are in truth to be used in serving the body of Christ. Paul affirms this truth when he says, "Through love *serve one another*" (Gal. 5:13). And also in these words: "But to each one is given the manifestation of the Spirit [spiritual gifts] *for the common good*" (1 Cor. 12:7).

Furthermore, if we could reduce serving the Lord to an act performed at a particular time and place, then this question arises:

Who are you serving when you *stop* performing that action? Do you cease serving the Lord when you leave the youth ministry, or the music ministry, or the single-parent ministry—or whatever context in which you carried out works of service? Obviously not. Serving the Lord, then, must mean something more than a deed we *do* at a specific time and place. Jesus said, "For even the Son of Man did not come to be served, but to *serve*, and to give His life a ransom for many" (Mark 10:45). Paraphrased, "I did not come so you could *do* something for Me; I came to *do* something for you." Again: God, always the giver.

The Truth about Serving the Lord

So what *does* it mean to serve the Lord?

Jesus said, "If anyone serves Me, he must follow Me; and where I am, there My servant will be also; if anyone serves Me, the Father will honor him" (John 12:26). To understand the serving of which He speaks, look at the preceding verse: "He who loves his life loses it, and he who hates his life in this world will keep it to life eternal." Jesus isn't asking us to perform for Him; He's asking us to *lose our lives* for His sake. So "serving the Lord" means we surrender our very lives to the fulfillment of His purposes, for His glory.

In this way we are to serve the Lord at all times, in every place, in every activity. We're serving Him whether we're hanging out at home, working out at the gym, or "putting out" at work. We serve Him as we follow Him, in every arena of life. Life outside serving the Lord doesn't exist, for life itself is lived in service to Him.

Listen to the apostle Paul: "Therefore I urge you, brethren, by the mercies of God, to present your bodies a living and holy sacrifice, acceptable to God, which is your spiritual *service* of worship" (Rom. 12:1). Whether you spend your day selling insurance, bagging groceries, overseeing a million-dollar company, managing a home, or leading a church, you're serving the Lord:

> Whatever you do, do your work heartily, as for the Lord rather than for men, knowing that from the Lord you will receive the reward of the inheritance. *It is the Lord Christ whom you serve.* (Col. 3:23–24)

When Paul wrote those words, he was thinking of slaves. Even they were to consider themselves as servants of the Lord.

So what does it mean to serve the Lord? It means giving your life—all of it—in accomplishment of His purposes, for His glory.

Summary

By the mercy and grace of God, we're to offer up our lives in service to Him. This is a life-encompassing surrender. As we surrender to Him, God pours out His blessings upon us. Once blessed, we're then able to serve (bless) others.

Through the blessings God bestows upon us, He displays Himself for His own glory. As Warren Wiersbe said, "A blessing is something God gives to us for our good and His glory."

But we miss out on this process of blessing when we try to "serve" based on the erroneous assumption that God needs our help, or that He wants a "payback" for all the good things He's done for us.

Do you want to live as a recipient of God's blessing? Do you want a life that blesses others? Do you want a life of *true* success? God longs to display Himself in and through your life, for your good and His glory. We can find no greater joy and no higher calling.

Where do you find the power to serve like this? Read on.

5

THE CREDIT HERESY

It had been forty days since Jesus' resurrection. His followers overflowed with indescribable joy as they mingled again with their risen Lord. What a swing of emotion from the afternoon when some of them had placed His lifeless body in the tomb.

Now everything was okay. How could it not be? Just like the good old days, sitting under His teaching, listening to Him speak of the Kingdom.

Little did they know what was coming.

As the book of Acts opens, we read that Jesus gathered His followers together and "commanded them not to leave Jerusalem, but to *wait* for what the Father had promised" (1:4). He'd spoken of this before, but now His words had added significance: "For John baptized with water, but you will be baptized with the Holy Spirit not many days from now" (1:5).

Puzzled, they asked, "Lord, is it at this time You are restoring the kingdom to Israel?" (1:6).

He answered,

> It is not for you to know times or epochs which the Father has fixed by His own authority; but you will receive power when the Holy Spirit has come upon you; and you shall be My witnesses both in Jerusalem, and in all Judea and Samaria, and even to the remotest part of the earth. (1:7–8)

This must have been confusing to them. Up to now they'd traveled little, and suddenly Jesus is talking about "the remotest part of the earth." What did He mean? Perhaps going somewhere remote sounded good compared to being witnesses in Jerusalem and Judea, where only a month earlier Jesus' own witness had resulted in His crucifixion. How would they fare any better?

They didn't have time for further clarification. "After He had said these things, He was lifted up while they were looking on, and a cloud received Him out of their sight" (1:9). Luke's next line must be one of the greatest understatements in all of Scripture: "And as they were gazing intently ..." That isn't hard to believe; their shock alone must have kept them "gazing intently" while they no doubt wondered, "Where's He going? What in the world's going on?"

To jar them from their skyward gaze, God sent angels appearing as "two men in white clothing" (1:10). "Men of Galilee," they boomed, "why do you stand looking into the sky? This Jesus, who has been taken up from you into heaven, will come in

just the same way as you have watched Him go into heaven"
(1:11).

While Luke doesn't elaborate, the disciples must have wondered, for at least a minute or two, "What now?" Reviewing Jesus'
pre-ascension instructions, they could remember only one directive: *Wait in Jerusalem for what the Father promised.*

Given their circumstances, to receive only one instruction
seems to fall far short of their need for direction. Let me try to put
this in perspective: As a father of three, I can remember when
MaryAnn and I would go out for an evening and leave our children
in the hands of a babysitter. Our three-hour absence required a fair
number of instructions. And on those rare occasions when we went
away overnight, MaryAnn would often leave *pages* of detailed directives and information.

But Jesus wasn't coming back in three hours, or the next day. He
was gone for good—after leaving *them* with the huge responsibility
of evangelizing and discipling the nations. And as far for being left
"safe and sound," this small band of Christ-followers was sur-
rounded by the same intense hostility that had instigated their
leader's execution only six weeks earlier. Talk about feeling alone!

And remember, they haven't read Acts 2. They don't know the
rest of the story. They know little about the Holy Spirit apart from
the brief description Jesus provided. What would the Holy Spirit
look like? How would they know when He arrived? What would
His power feel like? What would it mean to be a "witness"? Just
how many days was "not many days from now"? They had many
questions, no answers, and no one to ask.

But with all this swirling in their minds, they were told, quite
simply, "Wait."

United in Waiting

The fact that they decided to obey this command from Jesus is amazing. Their doing so was a remarkable demonstration of just how far their faith had come in the last forty days. "Then they returned to Jerusalem.... When they had entered the city, they went up to the upper room where they were staying" (1:12–13). We're told 120 were gathered there. Not exactly an overwhelming number.

And what did they do there?

They waited!

To these 120, *waiting* didn't simply mean hanging out: "These all with one mind were continually devoting themselves to prayer" (1:14). To *wait* meant they would *pray*.

Acts doesn't tell us what they prayed about, but it's safe to assume that at the heart of their prayers were three simple words: "Come, Holy Spirit." That was, after all, what they were waiting for, as Jesus had said: "Wait for what the Father promised." Nothing more.

The profound implication behind this single instruction is clear: *There's only one need at this time, and that's for the power of the Holy Spirit. Don't go anywhere—don't do anything—until you receive it.* Had they received a second instruction, they may have been tempted to skip the waiting (and the praying). But they couldn't afford to skip it, because everything that lay ahead was dependent on their receiving the Holy Spirit. So they must have prayed with fervor.

I find this to be no small thing, because for me, *waiting* for God is one of the most difficult dimensions of following Him. If you're like me, you don't wait well either.

It's significant that verse 14 tells us they "all with one mind were continually devoting themselves to prayer." Such a phrase communicates unity. Together—in *fellowship*—they were unified in their commitment to wait.

Hours of waiting turned into days. A week went by, and they were still waiting.

They ended up waiting ten days. It must have felt like an eternity. Why *did* God make them wait so long before sending the Holy Spirit? Scripture doesn't say. Perhaps He wanted to stretch their faith by testing their obedience. Waiting on God has a way of doing that; delay is one of His favorite tools as He works to make us like His Son.

The Result of Waiting

Finally the waiting was over. The Holy Spirit came:

> When the day of Pentecost had come, they were all together in one place. And suddenly there came from heaven a noise like a violent rushing wind, and it filled the whole house where they were sitting. And there appeared to them tongues as of fire distributing themselves, and they rested on each one of them. And they were all filled with the Holy Spirit and began to speak with other tongues, as the Spirit was giving them utterance.
>
> Now there were Jews living in Jerusalem, devout men from every nation under heaven. And when this sound

occurred, the crowd came together, and were bewildered because each one of them was hearing them speak in his own language. They were amazed and astonished, saying, "Why, are not all these who are speaking Galileans? And how is it that we each hear them in our own language to which we were born? Parthians and Medes and Elamites, and residents of Mesopotamia, Judea and Cappadocia, Pontus and Asia, Phrygia and Pamphylia, Egypt and the districts of Libya around Cyrene, and visitors from Rome, both Jews and proselytes, Cretans and Arabs—we hear them in our own tongues speaking of the mighty deeds of God." And they all continued in amazement and great perplexity, saying to one another, "What does this mean?" But others were mocking and saying, "They are full of sweet wine." (Acts 2:1–13)

The day of Pentecost provided the perfect setting for the 120 to be witnesses. They didn't need to travel to the nations after all; *God brought the nations to them*—"from every nation under heaven," verse 5 says. The sound produced by the coming of the Spirit attracted a crowd, and those filled with the Spirit were suddenly able to speak multiple languages, "coincidentally" matching those spoken by the spectators. The curiosity level of those looking on was off the charts.

Peter stood before this gathered throng. In an impromptu sermon he testified to the truth about Jesus:

Men of Israel, listen to these words: Jesus the Nazarene, a man attested to you by God with miracles and wonders and signs which God performed through Him in your midst, just as you yourselves know—this Man, delivered over by the predetermined plan and foreknowledge of God, you nailed to a cross by the hands of godless men and put Him to death. But God raised Him up again, putting an end to the agony of death, since it was impossible for Him to be held in its power. (2:22–24)

Peter concluded with his focus fully on Christ: "Know for certain that God has made Him both Lord and Christ—this Jesus whom you crucified" (2:36).

The crowd's response to his sermon was immediate and intense: "Now when they heard this, they were pierced to the heart, and said to Peter and the rest of the apostles, 'Brethren, what shall we do?'" (2:37).

While thoughtful preparation is usually wise before getting up to present God's Word, Peter's sermon obviously wasn't a result of such preparation. His words resulted from being filled with the Holy Spirit. The Holy Spirit was, in fact, the One speaking; Peter was simply the talking head. In the same way, the people were "pierced to the heart" not by Peter's eloquence or charisma, but by the Spirit's power.

Verse 41 sums up the fruit produced by this move of the Spirit: "So then, those who had received his word were baptized; and that day there were added about three thousand souls." This number gives us some idea of the size of the crowd that day, as well as the impact of the Holy Spirit's power. It's one of the few times a number is conveyed in the New Testament to indicate ministry impact.

In a single day, a few hours really, the group of Christ-followers in Jerusalem grew from 120 to about three thousand.

Jesus was right, after all; His followers needed just *one* instruction: *Wait for the Holy Spirit.* Nothing else mattered, because everything God does starts there.

On the night He was betrayed, Jesus had told His twelve disciples, "It is to your advantage that I go away; for if I do not go away, the Helper will not come to you; but if I go, I will send Him to you" (John 16:7). While those words must have sounded crazy at the time, Jesus knew from personal experience that the Holy Spirit—who John later describes for us as the "anointing" that "teaches you about all things" (1 John 2:27)—makes all the difference. Not only would Christ's followers have power, but the Spirit would show them what to do. *He* would answer the question, "What next?"

Jesus had given His followers only one directive. Now, with the Holy Spirit, additional directives would come.

A Familiar Pattern

If we turn back the clock about three and a half years before Acts 1, we can read about Jesus' own experience with the Holy Spirit at the beginning of His public ministry:

> Now when all the people were baptized, Jesus was also baptized, and while He was praying, heaven was opened, and the Holy Spirit descended upon Him in bodily form like a dove, and a voice came out of heaven,

"You are My beloved Son, in You I am well-pleased."
(Luke 3:21–22)

Note what Jesus was doing when the Spirit descended upon Him: He was praying, just as He'd instructed His followers to do. It's in response to prayer that heaven opens and the Holy Spirit's influence floods our lives. In this passage we again aren't told the content of the prayer, but in light of what occurred in the moments that followed, perhaps He, too, had prayed those three simple words: "Come, Holy Spirit."

Whatever He said, the Spirit did come. And what a difference He made!

Continuing in Luke, we read, "Jesus ... returned from the Jordan and was led around by the Spirit in the wilderness for forty days, being tempted by the devil" (4:1–2). Luke then records three powerful temptations the devil placed before Jesus, each of which He was able to withstand. From where did the power come to say no to them?

If you look in your own Bible at Luke 4:1 and compare it to my quote above, you'll notice I left out one small phrase: *"full of the Holy Spirit."* Jesus was *full of the Holy Spirit* as He was led into the wilderness. He was able to say no to Satan's temptations because of that fullness; that's where the strength came from. When Luke wrote his gospel under the inspiration of the Spirit, the Spirit made it clear that this phrase must be included.

After these temptations were over, we read this: "Jesus returned to Galilee ... and news about Him spread through all the surrounding district. And He began teaching in their synagogues and was praised by all" (4:14–15). His teaching was unlike any the

people had ever heard. He possessed an authority, a power, a ring of
truth that set His words apart.

But a closer look at your own Bible reveals that once again I've
left out a phrase. The verse actually says that Jesus returned to
Galilee *"in the power of the Spirit."* The power of the Spirit was the
reason Jesus' teaching had such authority and "was praised by all."

Wait, Then Cooperate

Jesus knew from His own experience that the Holy Spirit's power—
the anointing—makes all the difference. And so, when He gathered
His followers for His parting words, the message was clear: They
were to *"wait* for what the Father promised." How much clearer
could it be? *Wait for the Holy Spirit. Don't go anywhere until you
receive His power. Don't do anything without it.*

If Jesus were to stand before us today, would His instructions be
any different? I think not. Without the Spirit's power our efforts are
just that: *our* efforts.

The apostle Paul understood this. Listen again to his words in
Colossians 1:29: "For this purpose also I labor, striving *according to
his power,* which mightily works within me." The prophet
Zechariah puts it most simply: "'Not by might nor by power, but
by My Spirit,' says the LORD of hosts" (4:6).

We often hear of the power of prayer. Countless books and sermons have testified to it. While the intent of these writers and
speakers is good, their message is often misunderstood. The power
is not in the activity of prayer; the power is in the Holy Spirit.

We need to make a subtle yet important distinction here.

When we focus on the activity of praying, we're in danger of concentrating on the wrong things—the words we say, the length of our prayers, how often we pray, our prayer posture, etc. This can lead to the misconception that the release of God's power depends on us. *Did I do it right? Did I use the right words? Have I asked enough?*

If the activity of prayer itself assured the power of God, then the Pharisees would have been the most spiritually powerful people of their day. Yet Jesus taught His followers to *not* pray as they did (Luke 18:9–14).

The power of prayer is not in the action itself; it's in the Spirit. Prayer is simply the cry of the heart that invites the Holy Spirit to invade our lives.

Again, we aren't told *what* those gathered in the upper room prayed about. If their specific words were critical to the coming of the Holy Spirit, surely we would be informed so we could pray the same way. The truth is, God isn't listening to what comes from our lips; He's listening to what comes from our hearts. When the words "Come, Holy Spirit" reflect the cry of our hearts, heaven opens and the Holy Spirit descends.

The words of Jesus supports this:

> For everyone who asks, receives; and he who seeks, finds; and to him who knocks, it will be opened. Now suppose one of you fathers is asked by his son for a fish; he will not give him a snake instead of a fish, will he? Or if he is asked for an egg, he will not give him a scorpion, will he? If you then, being evil, know how to give good gifts to your children, *how much more will your heavenly*

Father give the Holy Spirit to those who ask Him? (Luke
11:10–13)

The 120 gathered in the upper room would be among the first
to test Jesus' promise. They waited for the Holy Spirit, then cooperated with His leading.

Wait, then cooperate. God wants it to be just that simple.

A Heart Cry Heard by the Spirit

I grew up attending South Park Church in Park Ridge, Illinois, a
suburb on Chicago's northwest edge. As a high school freshman in
1970, I joined the thirty or forty students who made up the
church's high school ministry. While the church numbered around
four hundred, we didn't have a youth pastor per se. Two young
married couples volunteered as leaders.

By the time I completed my freshman year of college in 1975,
that same youth ministry numbered twelve hundred and became
the launching pad for Willow Creek Community Church. In less
than five years I'd watched hundreds of students come to know
Jesus as their personal Savior. I saw lives transformed in ways I
never thought possible. The experience was as close to Acts 2:42–
47 as anything I've ever seen. What happened? How is that sort of
impact explained?

I trace the beginning all the way back to one Sunday evening in
Greg Roman's backyard on a late summer night, just before my soph-
omore year in high school. Our youth group had gathered, as usual,
following the church's Sunday evening service. On this particular

night we were gathered around a "campfire" in Greg's yard. The meeting was very informal, no program as such. We were just hanging out around the fire. The volunteer leaders hung out on the fringes, more as chaperones than leaders.

I don't remember how it started, but suddenly the conversation turned to unsaved friends. One by one, those present began to pour out their concerns for friends at school who didn't have a relationship with Jesus, classmates who were headed for hell for all eternity, friends who were trapped in sin, experiencing the consequences, and ruining their lives. Kids began to weep as they shared. Such emotion wasn't a common thing at our weekly gatherings. And it wasn't the result of some heart-wrenching testimony we'd just heard, nor a stirring message from God's Word. This emotion was a sincere response to a heartfelt burden for friends who were living apart from Jesus.

When the unrehearsed sharing died down, spontaneous singing began. I don't recall all the songs we sang, but I do remember singing "Pass It On," probably the top Christian song of its day, with this opening line: "It only takes a spark to get a fire going."

As I walked away that night, I knew—we all knew—that something unusual had taken place. We'd spent many Sunday evenings together, but none like this one. Nearly thirty-five years later, I can still remember where I was sitting in relation to others around that fire.

I believe God heard a heart cry that Sunday evening coming from Greg Roman's backyard. We have long forgotten the specific words we spoke, but not God's response to those words.

To confirm some of the details in this account, I called a friend who had also been present that night. He recalled the evening with even greater clarity than I just described. When God visits your life in an unmistakable way, you don't easily forget it, and I believe God visited our youth group that night and poured out His Spirit upon us. The tangible result was God's power for evangelism. It was for the salvation of our friends that we prayed, "Come, Holy Spirit."

A short time later the church hired a young man named Dave Holmbo to assist with the youth ministry. Dave was a musician, so he quickly formed us into a singing group he called the Son Company. Contemporary Christian music hadn't yet come into full view, so Dave would often change the lyrics of secular songs to make them "Jesus music." God had placed some musically talented kids in our group, so the sound we produced was pretty good. All we were missing was a drummer.

As we met for our weekly practice one Wednesday night, a young man walked in who recently had crossed paths with Dave. He was obviously new; with hair to his shoulders and a black leather jacket, he didn't look like the rest of us "church kids." His name was Mike Bourbon, and he came from the suburb of Palatine, about thirty minutes away. He'd just recently become a Christian, resulting in a major change in his way of life. To say he was excited about his newfound faith would be an understatement. Unlike us "church kids," Mike had experienced life apart from Jesus, so his new life in Christ put a smile on his face that never seemed to go away. Mike became our new drummer.

None of us knew anything about spiritual gifts at the time, but if we had, we would have known early on that God had given Mike the gift of evangelism. He had an anointing for it unlike anyone I'd ever known. To this day I've never seen a personal ministry of evangelism as fruitful as Mike's was over the next few years. By the spring of 1975, four school buses transported approximately 150 kids from Palatine to Park Ridge each Wednesday night—all a direct result of Mike's personal ministry of evangelism.

Cooperation with the Spirit Continues

Meanwhile our Wednesday evening Son Company singing practice lost its Bible study teacher. So Dave called an old friend he knew from his days with Awana Youth Association. Bill Hybels, a college student at the time, was sensing that the Lord wanted to take his life in a new direction, so he accepted Dave's invitation, relocated to the Chicago area, and began leading our Bible study.

A twenty-minute teaching time, led by Bill, followed an hour of music practice, led by Dave. On the heels of Bill's teaching, we would often break into small groups to discuss what he'd taught, then pray for one another.

Our group was falling more and more in love with Jesus and one another with each passing week. I wouldn't have labeled it as such back then—after all, I was a high schooler—but that's what was happening. And the burden for unsaved friends was growing even stronger. Many of us began to invite these friends to attend on Wednesday nights. The fact that we had singing practice first was a bit awkward. Our friends either sat in the back of the room listening as we practiced, or they hung out around the church until the Bible study began. These friends didn't come with Bibles, and they certainly weren't ready for a small-group discussion and prayer. In today's terms our Wednesday evening program was "seeker hostile." It didn't matter, however, as the Holy Spirit was present. As a result our friends were coming to know Jesus as their personal Savior.

Our little youth group began to grow in number: fifty, then sixty, seventy, eighty…. The small "fireside room" in South Park Church filled to capacity each Wednesday evening with kids hungry for God. We could see that Bill was not only gifted to communicate Bible truths in ways high school students could understand, but he also had the gift of evangelism.

(By the way, in the story I'm recounting here, you'll see me citing some numbers—but only as a detail in the whole picture, and certainly not as our focus or the ultimate measure of success. I trust you're already aware that a focus on numbers is in no way what I'm promoting.)

By the end of my junior year, Bill and Dave decided to move music practice to late Sunday afternoon and save Wednesday evenings for outreach. Wednesday night received the name Son City, and it was designed as the perfect setting in which to bring an unsaved friend to hear about Jesus.

I'll never forget the first Son City evening, when an invitation to receive Christ was extended, and a couple dozen kids came forward. A friend and I prayed with a first-time visitor named Mike Hoffner as Mike asked Jesus to come into his life. This was the first of many such prayer times.

By late 1974, Son City was meeting two nights a week to accommodate all the kids who were attending—from five to six hundred on Wednesdays and about the same number on Thursdays. Bill and Dave added "Son Village" on Monday nights to help these new believers, as well as us "older" ones, continue to grow spiritually.

In October 1975 we planted Willow Creek Community Church—in Palatine, where Mike Bourbon had come from three years earlier. Mike and his young fellow believers, along with a few of us from South Park, became Willow Creek's initial core group.

Giving Credit Where Credit Is Due

What caused this surge of spiritual responsiveness we witnessed in the early '70s?

I could tell you that Dave Holmbo's creative genius was responsible for the phenomenal growth, as he introduced contemporary Christian music, drama, and multimedia to our ministry before they were common elsewhere. I could say it was Bill Hybels' ability to communicate God's Word in ways that really connected with teenagers. I could credit the ministry strategy we employed, which focused on reaching the unsaved (we were holding a "seeker's service" long before that term became common ministry language). I could acknowledge all the "sharp" Christian kids at the core of our youth group who were also leaders on their high school campuses.

I could point to any or all of those factors as the "keys" to explain the explosion of life transformation that occurred during those few short years. But in doing so I would be overlooking the one true key that made those factors what they were—the anointing of the Holy Spirit.

The truth is, the Holy Spirit led Dave Holmbo to our little youth group at South Park Church and gave him the necessary gifts, passion, and insight that enabled him to use contemporary art forms to communicate the traditional gospel message. The Holy Spirit also led Bill Hybels to our group and gave him the spiritual gifts of teaching and evangelism that enabled him to communicate the truths of Scripture in a way that captivated the hearts and minds of high school students. By God's grace Dave and Bill cooperated personally with the Holy Spirit's leading in their lives. This same willingness to cooperate with the Spirit moved music practice from Wednesday to Sunday so Wednesday evenings could be devoted to outreach.

Likewise the Holy Spirit caused Dave Holmbo to cross paths with Mike Bourbon. While Mike proved to be a great drummer, the spiritual gift of evangelism, given to him by the Holy Spirit, proved to bear the greatest fruit. Mike repeatedly said, "Someday God is going to do something great in Palatine." And his words became prophetic as Willow Creek Community Church was planted in Palatine a few years later.

As I said above, by crediting human factors as the cause behind spiritual responsiveness, I'd be overlooking the one true key. While true, I'd actually be guilty of something far more significant: I would be robbing God of His deserved glory. To point to human factors as the explanation for what God accomplishes is heresy. To assign credit to man that rightfully belongs to God is a form of blasphemy.

Yet how quickly we seem to do just that. We lift up certain ministry strategies as "genius." We credit some individuals with being "so gifted." We label specific methodologies as "cutting edge." Even as I write, words such as "postmodern" and "emergent" are used as though our understanding of them is "the key" to ministry effectiveness. The truth is, certain ministry strategies are "genius" because the Holy Spirit designed those strategies. Individuals are "gifted" because that's what the Holy Spirit does. And He doesn't do it to "some"; He does it to all of God's people. To the degree that "some" see greater fruit as a result of using their gifts is due to the

Holy Spirit being at work through them, as He chooses. The Holy Spirit also brings new insights that result in "cutting edge" practices. As for "postmodern" and "emergent," the Holy Spirit's wisdom has always enabled God's spokespeople to connect with the culture of their day. We make a great error when we focus on the outcome of what the Holy Spirit does in a specific ministry or through a specific person and, as a result, try to copy that outcome in our life and ministry. This is why those three words, "Come, Holy Spirit," are so important—and why Jesus gave His followers just one instruction: "Wait for the Holy Spirit."

Hindsight affords us the opportunity to look back upon the early 1970s and see that God was pouring forth a spirit of evangelism upon youth all around the world. This outpouring was so significant that it has since been labeled "the Jesus Movement." While human factors obviously play a part in it, as God desires to work with and through His people, the Holy Spirit is the central factor in all that God does.

While Peter and the 120 played a part in what God did in that upper room, it would be a mistake of the greatest magnitude to credit them with what occurred. If we can credit them with anything, it's the fact that they were willing to wait—to pray—and then cooperate with the Holy Spirit's leading.

What Has Changed?

What has changed in the past two thousand years that should alter *our* approach to accomplishing the Great Commission?

Nothing! "Come, Holy Spirit" is still where it all begins.

Notice how Acts 2 begins with the coming of the Holy Spirit (2:4) and ends with this: "And the Lord was adding to their number day by day those who were being saved" (2:47). We must avoid the temptation to reverse the order of these two events. We make a huge mistake when our greatest thoughts and energy are given to number-building strategies. *How can we add more people?* becomes our chief concern and primary focus.

Having grown up in a strong evangelical background, I know my understanding of the Holy Spirit was severely lacking for much of my life. He was clearly the third person of the Trinity—in most cases, a distant third. I paid a price for this immaturity. I wish I'd appreciated the role of the Holy Spirit at a much younger age.

While I'm a big believer in ministry *strategy*, I've become an even bigger believer in the outpouring of the Holy Spirit. The best strategy, without the Spirit's anointing, is worth about as much as the paper it's written on. Acts 2 shows that God designed a strategy, centered around the Day of Pentecost, when men gathered from every nation under heaven and would return to their nations carrying the gospel. This strategy, carried out by the 120, reflected cooperation with the movement of the Holy Spirit.

Formulating strategy apart from the move of the Spirit is a waste of time. Copying other ministries' strategies because *they* saw fruit as *they* cooperated with the Spirit is an even bigger waste of time. If God had a specific formula involving three steps or eight principles or four keys, He surely would have given it to us in the New Testament. But He didn't. He said, "Wait." *Wait* for the anointing. *Wait* for the Holy Spirit. And once He comes, *cooperate with His* leading. We need to do the same!

Summary

No matter what your role in the work of the Kingdom of God may be, your ability to be faithful, fruitful, and fulfilled for the purpose of making God famous is dependent upon the anointing of the Holy Spirit.

This is the lesson we must learn from the earliest beginning of the church as we see it recorded in the book of Acts, as well as from the life of Jesus as seen in the Gospels. What was true then for them is true also now for us.

May we start every day—and every part of every day—with the heart cry, "Come, Holy Spirit." That's a prayer God answers every time.

Wait for Him, then *cooperate* with His leading.

6

THE ORGANIZATIONAL HERESY

If you've ever built a house, you know the importance of a good blueprint.

Over the course of our marriage, MaryAnn and I have lived in two different houses we designed and built. We can tell you from experience that you'll save yourself a great deal of time, money, and frustration if you minimize changes after construction begins. Change orders, as they're called, are expensive. They're also a hassle. Putting in the energy and research needed to come up with the right plan from the start is the far better plan. If the "final blueprint" proves indeed to be final, building a house is more enjoyable, less expensive, and much less stressful.

The same principle applies when trying to build a church. The right blueprint makes all the difference. If the organization is laid out according to New Testament specifications, the construction process is much more enjoyable and far less stressful. And most importantly, you'll end up with a church that really works.

In this chapter I want to lay out two different organizational models.

The Institutional Model

What I call the institutional model of church structure reflects what I've observed in my experience as a church consultant, as I've worked alongside those who labor diligently to build a church. I've found this model to be more the norm than the exception.

It can be described with the following four phrases (and I'll explain each one):

- Board Led
- Staff Run
- Congregation Served
- World Ignored

Board Led

The "institutional" church is "led" by a board. Depending on denomination or cultural context, this board goes by various names (elders, deacons, session, council, overseers, leadership team, consistory, etc.). Though the senior pastor is typically a member, and sometimes other pastors and staff are as well, this board is usually made up primarily of laypeople. They're either chosen by the congregation or appointed by a committee selected by the congregation. Board members typically serve for a term of two or three years.

The board usually meets once a month, with meetings lasting for several hours. If an emergency arises, members may schedule additional meetings. While the board meeting usually opens and closes with prayer, the majority of the time is spent discussing the administrative affairs of the church. These include finances, facilities, technology, personnel, putting out fires, and establishing policies intended to prevent future fires. By establishing policies and making decisions concerning these administrative matters, the board expresses its leadership in the life of the church or ministry.

Board members commonly see their role as that of being representatives of the congregation. Their job is to make sure the congregation's views are heard and their needs met.

Leadership on the board varies, depending on the senior pastor's makeup. If he's a "gifted leader" (an organization builder), he plays a central role in leading the board. Otherwise an appointed "chairperson" plays that key role. Either way, the institutional church or ministry looks to the board for leadership.

The effectiveness of their leadership is measured by the following:

- Are the church's finances in order?
- Do the facilities meet the ministry's needs?
- Are paid personnel doing what they should be doing? And are they adequately compensated for their efforts?
- Are the congregation's views being heard and attended to?
- Are the congregation's needs being met?

If the answers to these questions are positive, the board is serving its purpose.

Staff Run

The institutional church is served by its staff—the church's paid employees. (If you're paid for what you do in the church, you're on the staff; if not, you're a layperson or volunteer.)

Staffers are expected to do the work of the ministry. They teach and counsel, they lead worship and pray. They plan programs and coordinate events. They visit the hurting, maintain the facility, oversee the finances, fulfill secretarial duties, and so on. If a "fire" starts in their area of responsibility, they put it out. If something needs to get done, they do it. They have volunteers who assist them, but it's clear that "real ministry" is done by staff members. In fact volunteers are in place to help the staff fulfill their ministry; these volunteers don't really have a ministry of their own.

In the true institutional church, for example, hospital visits don't really count unless a staff person makes them, preferably an ordained pastor. An official pastor officiates funerals. Unless someone whose educational credentials and title speak of his or her qualifications provides counseling, it isn't *really* counseling.

Staff people in the institutional church are the hubs around which the wheels of ministry spin. They're seen as the primary providers of ministry service, and their effectiveness is measured by the following:

- Are the programs, services, events, and activities appealing to the congregation?
- Are the programs, services, events, and activities addressing and meeting the needs of those who attend?

▪ Are the programs, services, events, and activities attracting an ever-increasing number of attendees?

If all the answers are yes, staff members are serving their purpose in the life of the institution.

Meanwhile, although they carry significant responsibility for the work of the ministry, the institutional staff has relatively little authority in the life of the institution. They can make requests and suggestions regarding finances, facilities, personnel, and policies, but in the end, the board typically makes the final decisions on such matters.

Congregation Served

The institutional church is organized to serve its *congregation*, a body made up largely of consumers—people who attend a church because they like what it offers.

In this way the church has more in common with a health club than it does the New Testament body of Christ. Members' needs determine what staff the church hires and what services and programs it provides. Members will continue attending and paying their "dues" (tithes or offerings) as long as their needs are being met.

I call these members "Eberts and Roepers," after the famous movie critics. They attend the church's services and programs, then render a thumbs-up or thumbs-down.

They expend little or nothing to make the church's ministry possible, and if another church comes to town offering better services, these Eberts and Roepers have no trouble relocating.

This contributes to the competition between churches and fosters the little "k" kingdom mentality among church leaders. Some of the largest churches in America are the largest because of their ability to put on a four-star production each Sunday morning. Just as consumers crowd the box office to view four-star movies, consumers fill sanctuaries to attend four-star church services.

World Ignored

Consumers, by definition, are focused on their own needs, not the needs of others. Therefore the institutional church, with a congregation made up largely of consumers, ends up ignoring the world.

The institutional church has an inward focus. Services, programs, events, activities, staff members' time and energy, use of the facilities, church budget—all focus almost exclusively on the attending flock. That makes it nearly impossible for the church to have an impact on the unsaved world around it.

Perhaps this explains why 50 percent of the churches in America failed to add one person by conversion last year. It's difficult to reach people who are being ignored.

Evaluating the Institutional Model

Although the model I just described is more the norm than the exception, the term "institutional church" is an oxymoron. This model has almost nothing in common with the New Testament church, and to think that it does is to be guilty of organizational heresy. In fact, in many respects, it's diametrically opposed to the nature and work of the church in the New Testament.

Moreover, the institutional church isn't working—even for those who are part of it.

Board members are weary of putting out fires at meetings that last until the wee hours of the morning, and they're equally weary of spending time and energy on administrative matters having little to do with imparting God's presence and power to their church and community.

Staff people are tired of planning programs and coordinating events designed to meet consumers' needs. They're burdened by others' expectations and the corresponding endless to-do list. They're pulling out their hair, trying to make everyone happy—an impossible task within the institutional congregation, given the diversity of needs and desires. They try to motivate consumers to become contributors, but this ceaseless challenge leaves them exhausted.

Let me express here my opinion about the unhealthiness of a typical staff arrangement that combines heavy responsibility with minimal authority. This system is especially detrimental when the board has considerable authority but minimal responsibility for hands-on ministry. A board that isn't actively involved in the work of the ministry is not equipped to make wise ministry decisions. And staff people who carry a great deal of responsibility with only nominal authority often become resentful of those who do have the authority. It's also far more difficult to bring true accountability to people who don't have authority proportionate to their responsibility.

Members of the institutional congregation are also weary. The few active contributors are tired of doing 80 percent of the work, and those who remain consumers are unhappy because the programs and services are never quite everything they want them to be.

The institutional church is failing equally at fulfilling the Great Commission. In many communities the unsaved population doesn't even see the church as a relevant option for addressing the challenges they face in life.

It's not working for anyone, really—because God simply did not design His church to operate according to the institutional model.

We find it easy to point a finger of blame at church leaders who operate according to this model, but such finger-pointing is unfair. First, there's not a church in America, or anywhere else for that matter, that doesn't have some institutionalism going on. As long as imperfect people make up churches, this will be the case.

Second, it's simplistic to blame a distinct minority for the true and troubling condition of the majority. I've coached enough leaders within the institutional church to know they love the Lord with all their heart, soul, mind, and strength. I've seen how hard they work to fulfill the ministry God has given them. I've witnessed the love they have for their congregations. I know the burden they carry for the unsaved world surrounding their facilities. No one wants to leave the institutional structure more than they do.

Unfortunately that's easier said than done. Changing consumers into contributors is a major challenge—so major that only God can do it. Replacing an inward focus with an outward focus is also challenging, as is repositioning staff to function as equippers. And it's especially difficult to get the eyes of board members off of administrative realities and onto spiritual realities. Such changes won't happen easily, quickly, or without a clear understanding and conviction concerning the blueprint God gives us in His Word.

The Biblical Model

The biblical church structure can be described with the following phrases:

- Board Protected
- Staff Led
- Congregation Serving
- World Served

Board Protected

In the New Testament the church's "board" is referred to as "elders" (or "bishops" or "overseers"). Their name isn't important; their function is. They exist to protect the body of Christ, and their biblical role as protectors is clear.

In Acts 20, Paul meets at Miletus with the "elders" from the church in Ephesus. He expected never to see them again (20:38), so this would be his final charge to them. He tells them, *"Be on guard* for yourselves and for all the flock, among which the Holy Spirit has made you overseers, to shepherd the church of God which He purchased with His own blood" (20:28). He warns of "savage wolves" that would come, "speaking perverse things, to draw away the disciples after them"; so he admonishes these elders to "be on the alert" (20:29–31). A shepherd's primary role was to protect his sheep from all danger, and this is no doubt the role Paul has in mind here.

Peter uses this imagery when he tells elders, "Shepherd the flock of God among you, exercising oversight not under compulsion, but voluntarily, according to the will of God; and not for sordid gain, but with eagerness" (1 Peter 5:2). He again draws the analogy between a shepherd's role and an elder's: Protect the flock.

Likewise the writer of Hebrews charges the congregation, "Obey your leaders and submit to them, for *they keep watch* over your souls as those who will give an account" (13:17).

Read all the New Testament passages that speak of elders, and their role is clear: *Protect*. This implies that there's danger; elders must protect God's church *from* something. But what?

First, elders are to protect the body of Christ from false teachers and the doctrines they espouse (Acts 20:28–30; Titus 1:9). They're to provide for the teaching of sound doctrine. In this way elders are ultimately responsible for the ministry of God's Word in the church. This responsibility should not fall exclusively to the pastor or teaching team, as is so often the case. Elders should be deeply involved in the ministry of the Word. And while most may not be up-front communicators, they're to play an active role in discerning what's to be communicated. What is it God wishes to say to our church? What does He want to emphasize in this season of our church's life? The elders should seek the mind of God on these matters, alongside the senior or teaching pastor who's the main communicator.

Elders can also be extremely helpful in providing feedback on content that is taught. After almost every message I presented at Willow Creek, I received a brief page of feedback from one of the elders serving as a representative of the group. If I delivered the same teaching at multiple services, I received feedback after the first service so I could make any needed adjustments before the next. Our other teachers also received this feedback. I appreciated this critique (though it often contained some corrective input), because the encouragement, insight, and perspective were always valuable.

Of course the ministry of the Word isn't limited to the pulpit. Elders should be attuned to the content communicated through visual media, drama, music, and even announcements. They should keep their eyes and ears open all around the church. Elders are protectors of the truth among God's people, guarding against false teaching.

A second danger in the church that requires the elders' protection is that of sin and its consequences. God is big on purity—to see that, we need look no further than the church's beginnings. The church was still in its infancy when sin entered the camp: Ananias and Sapphira lied "not … to men but to God" (Acts 5:4), and their sin cost them their lives. God immediately took steps through Peter (an elder) to root out the sin and to send a message to the church that sin will be dealt with. As a result, "great fear came over the whole church, and over all who heard of these things" (5:11).

The Bible is clear throughout its entirety about God's position on purity and unity. Sin and division hinder the Spirit of God, so elders are called to guard the body against them. On a practical level, this means elders play a central role in exercising church discipline, thereby safeguarding the church from sin's consequences.

A third way that elders are to protect God's people is in times of difficulty or trial. This is done most often through prayer, as the apostle James instructs us:

> Is anyone among you suffering? Then he must pray. Is anyone cheerful? He is to sing praises. Is anyone among you sick? Then he must call for the elders of the church and they are to pray over him, anointing him with oil in the name of the Lord; and the prayer offered in faith will restore the one who is sick, and the Lord will raise him up, and if he has committed sins, they will be forgiven him. (James 5:13–15)

Although this unified, personalized prayer support isn't always feasible in larger congregations, elders should make every effort to be keenly involved in praying over those who are suffering. People should receive regular opportunity to come to the elders for prayer.

I believe a case can be made that elders are ultimately responsible for the prayer ministry of the church. While the task shouldn't be left exclusively to them, it's their responsibility to make sure the church is devoted to prayer. A praying church is indeed a protected church.

Fourth, the elders are to protect the work of the church. The church's mission is clear; Jesus spells it out in what we call the Great Commission:

> Go therefore and make disciples of all the nations, baptizing them in the name of the Father and the Son and the Holy Spirit, teaching them to observe all that I commanded you; and lo, I am with you always, even to the end of the age. (Matt. 28:19–20)

It is the elders' duty to ensure that the church is making every effort to fulfill the Great Commission. This board should be wrestling with questions like these: Is our church engaged as it should be with the surrounding community? Are we, as a body of believers, building relationships with those who are not yet members of God's family? Are we finding ways to present the gospel, in word and deed, to the people of our community? Are the ministries of our church reaching out to meet the needs that exist in people's lives outside our fellowship? Are we praying as a body for the salvation of others? The work of evangelism should be a front-burner issue for the board. This is the first dimension of the Great Commission.

The second dimension of the Great Commission—"teaching them to observe all that I commanded"—is often referred to as *discipleship*. The board is ultimately responsible for the church functioning as the body of Christ, with every member serving and being served as God intends (see 1 Cor. 12—14; Eph. 4:1–16; and Rom. 12 specifically). In this way, members grow in terms of spiritual maturity.

The focus of the church should be both inward and outward.

To measure the effectiveness of the elders (the board), a church should ask the following questions:

- Throughout the ministries, services, and programs of the church, is the teaching of the Word accurate, anointed, and applicable to life?

- Is the church covered and bathed in prayer?

- Can the Spirit move freely because we're united and free from the consequences of sin?

- Is the church operating as a true body, fulfilling its biblically stated purpose to one another and the unsaved world?

If the answer to each of these questions is yes, the board is serving as God intended.

An important note here: The board doesn't serve as representatives of the congregation. It's not their role or responsibility to represent the people's views or to guarantee that their desires are met. Elders are to serve as representatives of God to the people and to lead the people into obedience to what God says.

Picture Moses as he meets with God on Mount Sinai. He wasn't coming on the people's behalf to give God a list of their "Ten Desires"; he was there to receive for the people God's Ten Commandments. Moses then returned to the people to tell them what God said they were to do. In the same way, elders are to "meet God," hear what He has to say, then lead His people to obey it—because it's through obedience that their needs are met.

This kind of "representation" is different than what we see in many churches today. We've mistakenly sculpted ourselves after the representative model used by our government. It's a good model for government, but a poor one for the church. Jesus is the head of the church, for whom He gave His life; therefore we take our marching orders from Him. We're to fulfill *His* desires, not the people's. As we follow His leading, He'll protect and provide for His church. Elders—as His representatives—will protect and provide for the church on His behalf.

Now perhaps you're wondering about administrative matters. If elders focus their time and energy on everything I just outlined, who takes care of the organizational realities of finances, facilities, and so on that churches face today?

We're to do the same thing Peter and the apostles did:

> Now at this time while the disciples were increasing in number, a complaint arose on the part of the Hellenistic Jews against the native Hebrews, because their widows were being overlooked in the daily serving of food. So the twelve summoned the congregation of the disciples and said, "It is not desirable for us to neglect the word of God in order to serve tables. Therefore, brethren, select from among you seven men of good reputation, full of the Spirit and of wisdom, whom we may put in charge of this task. But we will devote ourselves to prayer and to the ministry of the word." The statement found approval with the whole congregation; and they chose Stephen, a man full of faith and of the Holy Spirit, and Philip, Prochorus, Nicanor, Timon,

Parmenas and Nicolas, a proselyte from Antioch. And these they brought before the apostles; and after praying, they laid their hands on them. (Acts 6:1–6)

The apostles saw to it that another group was raised up to address administrative demands that would take them away from the ministry of prayer and the Word. Their particular issue—serving the widows—is very different than our administrative issues today: finances, facilities, personnel administration (compensation benefits, insurance), technology, etc. But the principle remains the same: Delegate these matters to another group (deacons) who can manage them under the elders' authority. There are godly and gifted people who are fully capable of managing these administrative matters so the elders are free to do the work God has called them to do. Typically those most capable of overseeing such matters tend to be different in their God-given makeup than those most capable of shepherd-like protection. These "deacon types," who are impassioned about seeing the church function in an orderly fashion, are different than the "elder types," who are most ardent about matters of protection. Further, whenever "deacon types" get on the elder board, the elder board seems to take on an administrative focus.

Staff Led

The biblical church is led by staff—but not only *paid* staff, which is an institutional definition of the word. By "staff" I'm referring to anyone and everyone in the church who's being called upon to make an Ephesians 4:11 contribution—equipping gifts—to the church's life. Any individual who fulfills the role of an equipper is a leader. You'll probably need to call such folks something other than "staff," because of the entrenched understanding of that word, but their function is what matters.

Let leaders lead. And leading—as I've emphasized earlier in the book—means equipping. I encourage you to identify all the people in your church who are responsible for equipping the saints for the work of service, and to make them a part of your staff. You can call them *ministry leaders, team leaders, equippers,* or something else that describes their role.

Although "staff" is an institutional term, every church and ministry has some "staff" people (paid employees) who are *not* called to function as leaders in an Ephesians 4:11 context. That's not who they are by gifting, and it's not reflective of what they're being paid to do (their assigned jobs focus more on support or serving). Conversely every church and ministry has verse-11 leaders—"lay" leaders—who are unpaid and therefore not considered "staff." We've allowed money to be the determining factor for identifying staff, but money should never be a distinguishing factor in the body of Christ.

I have a friend named Sue who has led her church's women's ministry for years as a volunteer. Since her husband, Jim, owns a very profitable company, Sue doesn't need to be paid for her role at the church.

The ministry Sue leads is one of the largest and most effective in the church, and everyone affirms the leadership she has provided to women. Sue is an equipper—a biblical leader in every sense of the word. But because Sue isn't paid, she's not on the staff and is not invited to staff meetings. Although she has requested a workspace in the church facility of some kind—even a cubicle with a desk would do—none has been provided. The reason: "There's no room." Her request for clerical help in the form of a part-time assistant was also turned down ("There's no money in the budget"), so she must provide her own administrative assistance.

Meanwhile the women's ministry has grown to twice the size of the men's ministry led by the associate pastor—who has an office with a door, plus a full-time assistant.

These circumstances have been disheartening to Sue, even though she loves her church, supports her pastor, and feels called by God to the ministry she directs. On several occasions she has said to me, "Maybe I need to be paid, just so I can be considered a part of the staff."

Identify your leaders, your equippers—paid *and* volunteer—and do all you can to empower them to lead. Make clear to them that it's not their job to do the work of ten people, but to raise up ten people to do the work. Then let the church know who they are. Do everything you can as an organization to give these leaders the resources they need to do their job effectively, including a measure of authority consistent with the responsibility they carry. When leaders are identified based on maturity and gifting and challenged to function as equippers, an "institutional church" will begin to make significant strides toward becoming a biblical church.

When seeking to measure the effectiveness of the "staff" (as I define it), ask the following:

- Are those in leadership positions functioning as equippers?

- Are additional leaders being raised up and developed within the ministry?

- Is the ministry expanding because newly developed leaders are being deployed in additional leadership roles?

- Are more and more servers (those meeting needs) being identified, developed, and engaged in ministry service?

- Is the ministry increasing in its impact because more servers are actively involved in serving?

If you can answer each question with a yes, the staff is functioning as God intended it to. If not, you either have the wrong people, or you have the right people doing the wrong things.

Biblical leaders equip the servers for their work. This automatically results in the expansion of ministry.

Congregation Serving

The biblical church is organized to serve one another. It's a community that takes care of itself.

Listen to the apostle Paul:

> But to each one is given the manifestation of the Spirit for the common good. For to one is given the word of wisdom through the Spirit, and to another the word of knowledge according to the same Spirit; to another faith by the same Spirit, and to another gifts of healing by the one Spirit, and to another the effecting of miracles, and to another prophecy, and to another the distinguishing of spirits, to another

various kinds of tongues, and to another the interpretation of tongues. But one and the same Spirit
works all these things, distributing to each one individually just as He wills. For even as the body is one
and yet has many members, and all the members of
the body, though they are many, are one body, so also
is Christ. (1 Cor. 12:7–12)

Every member of the body of Christ has at least one spiritual
gift, and it's to be used to serve others. "As each one has received
a special gift, employ it in serving one another as good stewards
of the manifold grace of God" (1 Peter 4:10).

The body of Christ works as God intends only when every
believer sees himself or herself as a contributor, not a consumer.
But the very nature of how most of us "do church" seems to
undermine this function. As church members gather on Sunday
morning, more than 90 percent do so as consumers. They come
to receive what has been prepared by the 10 percent. This is in
stark contrast to what Paul writes: "When you assemble, each one
has a psalm, has a teaching, has a revelation, has a tongue, has an
interpretation. Let all things be done for edification" (1 Cor.
14:26).

How different would our church experience be if everyone
contributed something when we gathered together? Not only
would everyone receive much more, but all who took part would
be blessed by doing so, for "it is more blessed to give than to
receive" (Acts 20:35). Some would offer a teaching, some a word
of encouragement. Some would bring an offering above and
beyond their tithe. Some would offer physical assistance to those

in need. Some would prepare food or bring some other tangible gift to meet a need. The list goes on and on. Even the very act of praying and asking God to give us something to contribute would impact our hearts and minds as we headed off to "church." We would be better prepared to worship, better prepared to hear the Word, and even better prepared to serve. As a result we would all receive a greater blessing from our church experience.

The body of Christ should be visiting one another in the hospital. It shouldn't matter that someone with the title of "pastor" did or didn't come. If a pastor has a strong personal relationship with the one hospitalized, he'll visit that person regardless.

At a memorial service the people who play leading roles should be those who "did life" with the one who has passed on. Chances are, these people have the most to offer a grieving family.

And when someone needs counsel, small-group communities should provide greater degrees of it.

In short the biblical church is a serving army. And when measuring their effectiveness, these are the questions to ask:

- What percentage of our congregation is making God famous through their faithful, fruitful, and fulfilling ministry?

- What percentage is serving in areas of ministry that reflect their passion?

- What percentage knows and is using their spiritual gifts?

- Are pastors and leaders free to focus on using their gifts because others are using their gifts?

■ Are church members' needs being met by the community
of believers, rather than everyone looking to the institution's paid staff to meet their needs?

If you can answer these questions favorably, then you're a part of
a serving congregation. Consider yourself blessed; this is how God
designed the church to operate.

World Served

Finally the biblical church reaches out to impact—to serve—a lost
and hurting world.

It was true in the first church:

> Day by day continuing with one mind in the temple,
> and breaking bread from house to house, they were
> taking their meals together with gladness and sincerity
> of heart, praising God and having favor with all the
> people. And the Lord was adding to their number day
> by day those who were being saved. (Acts 2:46–47)

The first Christians in Jerusalem were obviously committed to
one another, yet this wasn't an inwardly focused church. They were
"having favor with all the people"—with those in the surrounding
Jerusalem community. This church was letting its light shine in the
lost and hurting world surrounding it, and the light shone so
brightly that those on the outside couldn't help but notice. Curiosity
got the best of them. And when they came to explore, a community

of people who cared engulfed them. The result was that "day by day" the Lord increased the numbers of "those who were being saved." Here was "The Church of Irresistible Influence," to borrow the title of Robert Lewis's book.

For years church leaders have increasingly asked, "What needs to be done to bring about more conversion growth?" The desire for the church to become a vehicle for evangelism has reached fever pitch. This is good! This explains why leaders have traveled long distances, at great cost, to churches like Willow Creek to attend conferences and learn more. They want to see their communities come to know Jesus.

How do we bring about a greater degree of evangelism? While people have written dozens upon dozens of books in an attempt to answer this question, I'm not sure it's any more complicated than this: Find a need and meet it. Our world has a need. The people of our communities have needs. The government can't meet all the needs. The agencies and social service organizations can't either. The greatest resource available to meet these needs is Jesus Christ, who works in and through His church.

Not long ago the church seemed to operate successfully under the motto "If we build it, they will come." We constructed beautiful facilities, put on great services, and ran effective programs—and people showed up. Many of them came to know Jesus. But now, for various reasons, this motto no longer seems to work as it once did. The lovely facilities don't have the same appeal. The services aren't fully able to address life's real issues. The programs don't go far enough to meet needs that run deep.

Given today's culture, the church needs a new motto: "If we go and meet their needs, they will listen." What needs exist in the lives of those in your community? Summon the resources of the church to address them, then bring those resources to the people in need. Any church that's actively making a difference in meeting the needs of the community will have "favor with all the people." As a result there's a good chance the Lord will add to *your* numbers day by day those who are being saved.

If you want to measure how you're doing in serving the world, answer the following:

- How many identifiable leaders do we have whose primary role is to equip the congregation to serve a lost world?

- How many people do we currently have whose primary ministry role is leading others to influence a lost world?

- What percentage of the overall budget do we spend to minister to those who are not yet saved, and who don't attend the church?

- What percentage of believers in the church has a regular and active participation in ministry focused on the community outside the church?

- What percentage of believers in the church (paid staff included) is actively building relationships with unsaved people?

The answers to these questions will probably affirm what you already know to be true about your church's impact in a lost and hurting world. If you're not satisfied with your answers, do something about it at once—so you can answer differently a year from now.

Summary

The church that's protected by the board, led by the staff, served by the congregation, and serving the world is operating as God has ordained. It's a church that will work and be a blessing to all.

Board members will be more than managers of human activity. They'll see that they're playing a critical role in a spiritual battle being fought before their very eyes.

Staff will know the joy of seeing God use those they've equipped to do the work of service. They'll then be free to focus on using the gifts God has given them.

Members of the body will discover it's more blessed to give than receive, as the Holy Spirit uses them to make a difference in someone else's life. They'll also discover that no endeavor is as exciting and fulfilling as building the Kingdom of God.

The board, the staff, and the body will delight in seeing people come to know Jesus as their personal Savior. As I said to a pastor friend recently, "Few things are more important to God's people than knowing He's at work in their midst." Isn't this what we all long for?

God has given us a blueprint for building His church. The closer we stick to it, the greater the results for all involved. Let's lead, teach, and pray in such a way that a biblical church is built. Leave its ultimate impact to God.

Paul wrote, "I planted, Apollos watered, but *God was causing the growth*" (1 Cor. 3:6). May we plant and water well, removing every obstacle to the growth God wants to bring.

PART TWO

A Return to Truth

7

LETTING GO OF LEADERSHIP HERESIES

You've probably seen research statistics such as the following (from Strategic Renewal International) that reveal startling and disturbing facts about the church in America today:

- Church attendance has decreased 9.5 percent in the last ten years, while the population has increased 11.4 percent.
- As many as 85 percent of churches have plateaued or are declining.
- Over the last fifteen years $500 billion has been spent on ministry, with no appreciable growth in the impact of the church.

If it's true that past performance is the best predictor of future results, then our results prove we can't continue to operate as we currently are. If we want more of God and more fruit for His glory, embracing *change* is our only option—however unpleasant the notion may be.

Let me say from the start, the changes I'm referring to are not primarily programmatic or methodological. We will not win the day by varying our ministry style, altering our music menus, shifting our focus from believer to seeker (or vice versa), or making postmodern adjustments. While these external changes can make some difference, we're in greater need of internal transformation.

This internal transformation begins with letting go of the heretical beliefs that hurt us and the ministries we lead. We need to look beyond the world's definition and understanding of leadership. We need to forsake our focus on achieving numerical "success." We need to throw away distorted notions and misconceptions concerning "serving the Lord." We need to abandon practices that are turning us into people we don't like and don't want to be. We need to discard the belief that ministry methods and techniques are the single most important factor for achieving greater effectiveness. We need to reject the institutional model that makes us look more like a health club than the body of Christ, and the institutional thinking that places unhealthy levels of responsibility on ministry "professionals" and prevents everyone else from functioning as God intends. We need to let go of everything that prevents God's people from experiencing the zone of His anointing.

All this will require change—a leadershift—that calls you to embrace a biblical definition and understanding of leadership: "Equipping others, using the gifts God has given you." *(How liberating is that?)*

This leadershift will enable you to evaluate your success using God's stated criteria. *(How freeing would that be?)*

It will put you in a position to receive the blessings of God. *(How much do you want and need His blessing?)*

It will help you experience the truth of God's word to Zechariah: "'Not by might nor by power, but by My Spirit,' says the LORD of hosts" (4:6). *(Don't you long to be caught up in a movement of God's Spirit?)*

It will assist your church or ministry to function as God outlines in His Word. *(Don't you long to be a part of an Acts 2:42–47 ministry?)*

The leadershift of which I'm speaking starts on the inside. It all begins with what we think and believe. Listen to Paul's words: "We are destroying speculations and every lofty thing raised up against the knowledge of God, and we are taking every thought captive to the obedience of Christ" (2 Cor. 10:5). This is exactly what we need to do.

Even the necessary organizational changes must begin on the inside. External changes, apart from internal conviction, are cosmetic at best and won't last. How many times have I seen a church change the format of its Sunday service because of what's working at the church across town. Changing the look of something doesn't change the heart of it. I've consulted many pastors who believed a "seeker service" would attract and reach unbelievers. Later, in frustration, they call wanting to know why it's not working. They claim their seeker service is as good as another one elsewhere that *is* working; yet not only are they *not* reaching unbelievers, but their believers are upset because they aren't being fed. A deeper look reveals that their church lacks a heart for the lost. These pastors end up learning the hard way that programs alone don't reach people; *people* reach people.

Every pastor knows that growing a heart for evangelism in the church is far more difficult than creating an evangelistic program. In the same way, moving from an institutional model to a biblical model requires nothing less than a move of the Holy Spirit, since we all, by nature, enjoy being served. We need a change of heart to drive any change of structure. A move away from institutionalism will happen naturally when people gain a heart's desire to be part of a church as described in the New Testament. And people who plan programs and coordinate events will not suddenly become equippers just because you call them leaders. Positions and titles are external and will accomplish nothing without a revolution of heart and mind concerning the role of leadership.

Just saying we need change is a far cry from making it happen. So how *do* we bring about this change of heart?

For starters we need to understand a very simple and important fact: *Without discontent, change will not happen.* We must be dissatisfied with things as they are. In fact the greater the change desired, the greater the discontent required for that change to occur. For example, losing five pounds requires only a minimal change in one's lifestyle, therefore minimal motivation (minimal discontent) is required. Losing fifty pounds, on the other hand, demands a lifestyle overhaul requiring significant motivation (significant discontent). The greater the discontent, the greater that motivation for change

Recently I asked a group of elders to rate their current contentment level with their church, using a scale of 1 to 10 (10 = "I'm really content with the church as it is"; 1 = "I'm deeply discontented and want to see immediate change"). The average of their responses was 8.5, with none lower than 8. My work with this church was done. It would be next to impossible to bring any change to an organization whose leadership says, "We're content with things as they are." This church had no need for change, at least not as far as these elders were concerned. There was just not enough discontent to change anything.

So where does discontent come from? I know of two sources.

Source 1: Pain

The first is *pain*. Yes, you read it right—pain. Pain is by far the greatest motivator for change. Nothing drives change like pain.

We see athletic teams make personnel changes because of the pain of losing. Businesses make changes in leadership or in product handling because of the pain of financial loss. Private schools, dependent on tuition income, make changes because of the pain of declining enrollment. And individuals make lifestyle changes because of the pain associated with strained relationships or declining health. Hearing the doctor say, "Lose weight and start exercising if you want to see your child graduate," produces enough mental and emotional pain (internal motivators) to inspire even the biggest couch potato to get into the gym (external behavior). The spouse who says, "You're married to your work, so I want a divorce," initiates enough pain to instigate a change in priorities.

Pain has a way of getting our attention. It's the ultimate reflection of discontent. As you could probably tell in reading my story in chapter 2, I was experiencing pain within the context of my ministry involvement at Willow Creek. That pain (discontent) drove me to consider and ultimately make changes I would have otherwise avoided.

While we usually think of pain as bad, it can often accomplish much good. A business losing money is a bad thing, so the pain that drives changes that result in increased profit is a good pain. Losing is bad for an athletic team, so the pain that drives them to make adjustments that bring victory is a good pain. And the pain produced by a bad doctor's report often yields lifestyle modifications that not only lengthen one's life but also improve its quality.

A church failing to see anyone come to Christ ought to be in pain over that fact. The church whose worship experience is lifeless and apathetic should also be in pain with that condition. And the church with 20 percent of its people doing 80 percent of the serving should be in pain over that reality. These are examples of the "good" kind of pain, and the resulting discontent should provide the needed motivation to drive change. This pain produces what I like to call "godly discontent." This is a discontent that the Holy Spirit generates within us when our experience doesn't match God's will.

The emotional, mental, and spiritual pain associated with ministering in the flesh ought to drive us to discover the zone of God's anointing, and then to make changes accordingly. Having children who are estranged from God and His church ought to produce enough pain to cause us to do whatever is necessary to reverse the situation. Working sixty to seventy hours a week to the demise of one's health and family should generate enough discontent to bring a change in priorities. And life as a self-serving consumer should produce a pain called emptiness that causes us to reconsider what's really important. Pain drives change like nothing else.

While you can apply this truth to every arena of life, this book is about the work of God's Kingdom. In this regard, how content are you? On a scale of 1 to 10 (1 = "painfully discontented"; 10 = "peacefully contented"), how content are you ...

with your current role in ministry? _____

with your sense of being faithful? _____

with your degree of fruitfulness "internally"? _____

with your degree of fruitfulness "externally"? _____

with your level of fulfillment? _____

with the measure of God's anointing you're experiencing? _____

with the church or ministry you're engaged in? _____

with the overall fruitfulness of that church or ministry? _____

Do your answers indicate any measure of "godly discontent"? What changes do you desire to make as a result? Is your discontent (pain) great enough to drive those changes?

Take a few minutes to consider those questions before reading on.

Source 2: Vision

Discontent comes from a second source as well, and we must turn to this source when pain *should* be felt, but isn't.

I'm referring to vision. *We become discontent with things as they are when a new vision creates a picture of something better.* What *is* becomes no longer acceptable in light of what *could be.*

One of the most dramatic and well-known examples of how vision generates discontent is Martin Luther King Jr.'s "I Have a

Dream" speech. In it he cast a vision of what *could be*—America as a sweet land of liberty—if we lived up to its creed and truly believed that all people are created equal. By the time he finished speaking, King's audience and much of America responded, "Yes! *Yes!* That's the America we want." Suddenly what *was* was no longer acceptable. A new vision described what *could be*, and it generated enough discontent to propel the civil rights movement forward in America. The change, though much needed, wasn't easy. It never is. And it seldom happens quickly, especially significant change.

At many times in life, we should be discontent, but we're not. We should be in pain, yet we're at peace. We become comfortable with what is. In such cases we need a new vision. We need to see someone paint a picture of what *could be* so we become dissatisfied with what *is*.

A church filled with consumers (Eberts and Roepers) may be content with employing a staff that works to meet their every need. Simply telling them to be discontent won't make them so. Shaming them won't work either. They need a new vision of what the body of Christ is to be … a picture of what *could be*. And until they get it, any programmatic or structural changes you implement are in vain. Only a new vision for what *could be* will generate a godly discontent with what *is*.

To get a new vision, we need look no further than the Word of God. All the vision we need for what *could be* is in its pages. In His Word, God gives us a vision of His church. And when we see that His vision doesn't match our condition, the resulting godly discontent should motivate us to change. This discontent may not be felt by 100 percent of those who need change (it probably won't be), but enough people need to feel it to drive the changes that produce different results.

This brings me to the next question concerning change: *How does change actually take place?*

I want to walk you through four steps that I believe will help facilitate change. These steps will help generate the good kind of pain as well as capture a new vision for what could and should be.

Step 1: Pray Fervently to Access God's Presence and Power

"'Not by might nor by power, but by My Spirit,' says the LORD" (Zech. 4:6). The Holy Spirit is the ultimate power behind all godly change. He's the definitive change agent.

Because this is true, we must always start with prayer. In any area where change needs to occur, ask for an outpouring of the Spirit. If your church lacks a heart for lost people, you need a change of heart. If your church lacks of a spirit of worship, you need a change of spirit. If your church is apathetic regarding prayer, you need to have your apathy arrested. If your church is filled with Eberts and Roepers, you need a change of desire.

Changes of heart are God's specialty. And since you and I can't change hearts, we need the Spirit of God to be poured *into* the hearts of God's people. The Spirit will sow discontent in the hearts of God's people when "what is" conflicts with "what God wants." The seeds of change are planted here.

We need to pray to this end. Along these lines I find great encouragement in a couple of specific passages.

The first:

> So I say to you, ask, and it will be given to you; seek,
> and you will find; knock, and it will be opened to you.
> For everyone who asks, receives; and he who seeks,
> finds; and to him who knocks, it will be opened. Now
> suppose one of you fathers is asked by his son for a fish;
> he will not give him a snake instead of a fish, will he? Or
> if he is asked for an egg, he will not give him a scorpion,
> will he? If you then, being evil, know how to give good
> gifts to your children, how much more will your heav-
> enly Father give the Holy Spirit to those who ask Him?
> (Luke 11:9–13)

That last statement from Jesus contains a powerful promise we
need to claim: The Father gives the Holy Spirit to those who ask.
The second passage is this one:

> This is the confidence which we have before Him, that,
> if we ask anything according to His will, He hears us.
> And if we know that He hears us in whatever we ask, we
> know that we have the requests which we have asked
> from Him. (1 John 5:14–15)

From the start we need to know that the change we're seeking is
in line with God's will. If this is true, we have promises here to claim:
"He hears us," and "we have the requests."

God's will is that all His people be involved in the work of His
Kingdom. His will is also that we know and use our spiritual gifts

in serving one another. And God's will is for each of us to be a success, as He defines it. Therefore any prayer for an outpouring of the Holy Spirit so that His people have His heart for serving is a prayer we know He will answer.

We can't afford to be guilty of what we read in James 4:2: "You do not have because you do not ask." So ask! Ask for an outpouring of the Holy Spirit concerning the change you want to see in the hearts of those who need it. And don't stop asking until He has answered your request. Pound heaven's gates until they open to you. If you grow weary or become discouraged in the process, read and meditate on Luke 18:1–8, and know that *no one* wants a biblical church more than God Himself. No one wants you and your brothers and sisters in Christ to minister in the zone of His anointing more than He does. And no one desires more greatly than God to see service that makes Him famous.

So pray—fervently—to access God's presence and power concerning the change you want to see take place.

In the early years of Willow Creek, it became apparent we needed to develop a disciple-maturing ministry. We were seeing significant numbers of people coming to faith in Christ, so the church was filled with newborn babies, spiritually speaking. While we strongly encouraged these new believers to attend the Wednesday evening service called "New Community" for additional feeding, we knew they needed more. They needed a relationship with a more mature believer who could guide them in their newfound faith. We needed to develop a small-group ministry. (This was before small-group ministry became as common in the church as it is today.)

In developing this new ministry, prayer was our first step. I went to approximately twenty people who I considered mature in the faith and asked them to join me in praying for the development of this new ministry. I invited them to join me in my office at six o'clock every Friday morning to pray for this new ministry, and to commit to praying personally for it on a regular basis. All twenty agreed to pray for the coming year.

So on Fridays we prayed for God to raise up leaders. We prayed for individuals by name. We prayed for young believers to feel a burning desire to be discipled. And we prayed for wisdom in structuring the ministry. I also put together a weekly prayer request list that these prayer partners could take home with them and continue to pray through personally.

To no one's surprise those twenty people ended up becoming key leaders in this new ministry. They were the ones to start the small groups aimed at discipling new believers. Then God raised up other leaders. God also brought others, already matured, from other places in the community and country.

For decades Willow Creek has had a thriving small-group ministry at its core. To this day thousands of people participate in organized small groups. God answered the prayers of those twenty people many years ago.

I encourage you to find your own twenty, or ten, or five prayer partners to join you in asking for an outpouring of the Holy Spirit concerning the change you want to see. When the Spirit begins to move in your midst, you'll have the very presence and power of God on your side. People's normal resistance to change becomes about as strong as tissue paper in the face of God's presence and power. His presence and power come in response to prayer.

Step 2: Teach God's Word *to Make His Will Known*

Romans 12:2 is a verse about change:

> And do not be conformed to this world, but be transformed by the renewing of your mind, so that you may prove what the will of God is, that which is good and acceptable and perfect.

Paul's word here for "change" is *transformed.* We need to be transformed because conformity to the world is unacceptable.

How does transformation occur? "By the renewing of your mind." Your current thinking will lead only to conformity—what Zig Ziglar calls "stinkin' thinkin'." As God's people we need to let go of all thinking that fails to match the truth of God's Word. As Paul says, we need to experience the renewing of our minds. Such new and different thinking will lead to a lifestyle that will "prove what the will of God is, that which is good and acceptable and perfect."

Once we've invited God to send forth His Spirit to provide the power for change, we need to teach His Word so His people understand His will. What is His will concerning those who are spiritually lost, and His will for believers in reaching them? What is His will concerning worship? Regarding prayer? What is God's will concerning the use of our financial resources (or rather, *His* financial resources entrusted to us)? What is His will for how we function as the body of Christ and as individual participants in the work of His Kingdom? The teaching of God's Word is intended to make His will known.

In many cases God's people simply don't know His will for their lives. It's not that they're unwilling to obey, but that they're ignorant. Making God's will known to them is the responsibility of leaders, specifically those with gifts of teaching and pastoring. And to the degree that our lives, individually or as a church body, do not reflect the will of God, we need to change—period! When His will is not being fulfilled, change becomes a mandate.

When working with leaders, I encourage them to consider what they want to see happen in light of God's will. *Should we be an evangelistic church?* No debate there. *Should we be a praying church?* Another no-brainer. *Should we make worship a priority?* Hmm. *Should we be generous with our resources? Do we really need to know and use our spiritual gifts? Should everyone be involved in the work of service?* Anyone wanting to debate these questions debates with God Himself.

While this seems like an obvious course of action for a leader, believe it or not, God's will is often given little consideration. Leaders become so focused on what *they* want to see happen that they run right past the most basic of questions: Is this in line with the will of God? Does His will support what I desire to see happen?

Asking this is especially critical when what we want to see happen requires change. As a general rule people resist change. Most of us tend to do "conformed" a whole lot easier than we do "transformed." If you can't support your plans by God's Word, you'll have a fight on your hands. No matter how logical your argument for what *you* want, people opposed to change will debate and wrestle against it. Their debate is almost always more emotional than logical, and debating someone's feelings is next to impossible.

To avoid this scenario, the leader must know and make clear that *God* wants a change to occur. It must be God's plan, not mine.

Some reading this book may not embrace the idea of spiritual gifts and would want to debate the concept with me. But it isn't my debate to have, for spiritual gifts didn't originate with me. I would encourage anyone who thinks that way to meet with God in His Word on the matter.

I believe that what I've written in this book can be supported by God's Word, and is therefore in line with His will. I've tried throughout the text to support my thoughts with Scripture. In light of this, the only debate you and I could have concerning this content is with my interpretation of God's Word. If my interpretation is accurate concerning the work of His Kingdom, we have nothing to debate.

So teach the Word so God's people will know His will. If change is called for, and the people know God is the one calling for it, their implementation will be made with His motivation. That doesn't mean the change won't be difficult; even under the best of circumstances, a measure of pain accompanies any change. In fact experts on the subject of organizational change encourage leaders to come up with a "pain plan" that identifies who will feel the pain of change and how they'll feel it. We can then be more prepared to address the pain brought on by change. Such pain will be more bearable when people know God is behind the change ... so teach His Word to make His will known.

Step 3: Lead by Example *to Provide Illustration*

"A pupil is not above his teacher," Jesus tells us, "but everyone, after he has been fully trained, will be like his teacher" (Luke 6:40).

Paul echoed this profound and practical truth throughout his writing. In 1 Thessalonians 1:5–7, he writes of the power of example:

> For our gospel did not come to you in word only, but also in power and in the Holy Spirit and with full conviction; just as you know what kind of men we proved to be among you for your sake. You also became imitators of us and of the Lord, having received the word in much tribulation with the joy of the Holy Spirit, so that you became an example to all the believers in Macedonia and in Achaia.

He repeats this theme in 2 Thessalonians 3:7: "For you yourselves know how you ought to follow our example, because we did not act in an undisciplined manner among you." And he encourages Timothy: "Let no one look down on your youthfulness, but rather in speech, conduct, love, faith and purity, show yourself an example of those who believe" (1 Tim. 4:12).

If we want a church where serving is gift-based and passion-driven, we need to model it. This means our own serving must reflect our gifts and passions; we need to be in the zone of God's anointing. When the work calls for a spiritual gift we don't possess, we should make every attempt to find someone else with the needed gift. While such an approach at first may sound unspiritual, in reality it is deeply spiritual. By calling on others, we apply the principle of equipping, while demonstrating our belief in the priesthood of all believers and the Spirit's distribution of gifts.

While at times all of us need to step out of our zones to meet a need, those times should be the exception, not the rule. The work of service doesn't need the best we have to offer in the flesh; it needs the best we have to offer in the Spirit. Those who are sick or hurting need the ministry of someone who has spiritual gifts like encouragement, mercy, and healing, not someone with the title "pastor" and the gift of evangelism.

Many large churches employ a "pastor of the day" strategy to meet pastoral care needs that arise. As situations of need occur, staff people take turns meeting them. For some being the pastor of the day is a joy because the job reflects their gifts and passion. They're in their zone. Others are equally unenthusiastic about it; they hope (sometimes pray) that they don't get called. I've even known some to trade days or pay other staff in some way to cover for them. The longer this misguided approach to congregational care is used, the harder it becomes to put a gift-based, passion-driven approach into effect. It's not being modeled.

At Willow Creek our original staff was neither gifted nor impassioned in counseling, so one of our earliest hires was a counselor. This was actually an act of mercy toward the people of the church, who would otherwise have been subjected to a "here's three steps to getting healthy, now go fix yourself" approach to counseling. As the church grew numerically, we found it impossible to hire enough counselors to meet the need. We then had to implement a completely different strategy, which included both trained lay counselors and an affirmed resource pool of outside professionals. In this way people received counseling from those both inside and outside the church who were gifted, impassioned, and trained for the role. Those who weren't "wired" to counsel were free to focus on what they *were* wired to do.

We also need to highlight examples of those who are ministering in their anointed zones. One time we had a man stand before the congregation and talk briefly about his spiritual gift of giving. He wasn't naturally comfortable speaking, so he gave his testimony with reluctance. As he spoke, his passion and commitment to use his gift showed. With matter-of-fact humility, he told the church that during the previous year, he and his wife had given 77 percent of their income to the work of the Lord. While many would quickly forget a general teaching on the gift of giving, this man's personal example left a lasting impression. Regardless of how much money he earned, 77 percent reflected a significant chunk of income. His and his wife's example was a powerful encouragement to our entire church family, and especially to others with the gift of giving.

Model the change you're trying to produce. Ask others to share testimonies that present a picture of what could be. Tell true-to-life stories, particularly before-and-after accounts. Find ways to apply the right practices, and put an end to practices such as "pastor of the day" that reinforce the wrong way of doing things.

About Step 4

I mentioned four steps showing us what needs to take place for change to occur, and we've looked at three of them:

Pray fervently to access God's presence and power.
Teach God's Word to make His will known.
Lead by example to provide illustration.

The Holy Spirit's movement, combined with the truth of God's Word and the power of example, serves to generate a great deal of energy for change. In the face of such movement, true believers will find it difficult to remain resistant to change. Most believers respond with desire to be a part of what God is doing. How can they not? God is in it!

In facilitating this change, one last step is critically important—so much so that I want to save it until this book's final chapter, so that we end with it.

Meanwhile let's look in the coming chapters at some key biblical truths that can dramatically alter the way we live and lead.

8

THE BLESSING FACTOR

"Twenty percent of our people are doing 80 percent of the work. How do we get more people to serve? We have so many who just *attend*. Getting them to move out of the stands and onto the field is a constant challenge. We've tried *everything*: promotions, personal testimonies, pleas for help, videos showing what God is doing— even threatening to shut down certain ministries if we don't get more help. Do you have any new ideas?"

I've heard these words more times than I care to count, from almost every ministry I know of. Very seldom do I visit a church or parachurch ministry and hear, "We have so many willing servants, we don't know what to do with them!" (Such a ministry would probably be called Fantasy Land.)

Why the shortage of workers?

While there's no one simple answer, one stands out above the rest: "They just don't get it."

What don't "they" get? They don't get the "blessing factor." The idle 80 percent don't get the fact that God wants to pour His blessings out upon them through *their* involvement in the work of His Kingdom. If they really understood this, they would be lined up to get involved.

From where they sit, involvement in God's work means high cost and little benefit. Already overextended with the cares of life, they have little time or energy to "put out" any more. They think that those leading God's work, and God Himself, just want to take more out of them. So they've become immune to convicting pleas for help.

What they need to understand is the "blessing factor." The truth is, when Kingdom work is done God's way, the benefits far outweigh the cost. Instead of making guilt-producing appeals for help, we need to help God's people understand that the blessings of God far exceed anything they could give.

Blessing 1: Friendship with God

Mark and I hadn't spoken in nearly a year. Living in different states, along with the general busyness of life, had made regular contact difficult. Nevertheless, all it took was my greeting—"Hey, Mark, this is Donzi" (his nickname for me)—and we made an immediate connection.

For the next thirty minutes we caught up with each other's lives and reminisced about the good old days. As always, Mark had me belly-laughing more than once. We felt no strain in the conversation. It was as though we were still doing life together as we had years before.

Our friendship began the summer following our freshman year in college. Mark had become a Christian that year, and our common involvement in the Son City youth ministry brought us together. For the next eighteen years we spent a lot of time in each other's company. We played softball and flag football on the same team each summer and fall. Every winter we took a ski trip out West with the guys. We belonged to the same gym and challenged each other to stay in shape. (You could see Mark enjoyed weight-lifting; you could also see I didn't.)

While we naturally enjoyed each other's company, our common passion for Jesus and the work of His Kingdom fueled our relationship. While Mark was a marketplace guy for the most part, he served briefly in a part-time capacity on the youth ministry staff at Willow Creek and was one of my main men. No matter what the ministry, I wanted Mark on the team. As a result we spent many hours together discussing ministry, brainstorming how we could be more effective, praying with and for each other, celebrating victories, encouraging each other in our respective roles, and of course laughing whenever possible. With weekly meetings, leadership training sessions, retreats, outreach events, and a host of other activities, we spent a great deal of time working side by side in ministry—all of which powered our friendship.

This is true in any work setting, isn't it? Working alongside someone can fuel a friendship.

The same is true in our friendship with God. And this is what God is after—a *friendship*. While He doesn't need our participation to accomplish His work, He *wants* our participation, because He wants *us*. He wants to work side by side with *you*, to do life with you. Jesus said, "No longer do I call you slaves, for the slave does not know what his master is doing; but I have called you friends, for all things that I have heard from My Father I have made known to you" (John 15:15).

I spent many years in ministry feeling as though God called me into a relationship with Himself just to put me to *work*. I now understand that *God calls me to His work in order to strengthen our relationship*. While God could accomplish His purposes without you and me, He desires to accomplish His purposes *with* you and me. The friendship, the companionship, the very presence of God with us—what a blessing!

This has been the case ever since the veil separating God's people from His presence was torn in two (Matt. 27:51). As the writer of Hebrews states, "We have confidence to enter the holy place by the blood of Jesus" (10:19). Because of the blood of Jesus, you and I can dwell in the presence of God. There's no greater expression of friendship than dwelling together.

To truly accomplish His work through us, God *requires* this friendship. It isn't optional. Jesus makes this clear:

> Abide in Me, and I in you. As the branch cannot bear fruit of itself unless it abides in the vine, so neither can you unless you abide in Me. I am the vine, you are the branches; he who abides in Me and I in him, he bears much fruit, for apart from Me you can do nothing. (John 15:4–5)

All our serving must flow from the blessing of His friendship.

Picture Jesus walking the streets of Jerusalem on a warm and sunny July day. He decides to swing by the pool called Bethesda. As usual, it's filled to capacity—not with swimmers, but with the sick, the lame, the blind. As always, they're waiting for the angel of the Lord to stir the waters. They never know the day or the time, but during certain seasons, an angel of the Lord comes to stir the pool's water with God's healing power. When he does, the first person in the water is healed.

Those who are quick on their feet have the clear advantage. The disabled are certainly at a great disadvantage. Such is the case with one man who has been lame for thirty-eight years (as the story unfolds in John 5:1–15).

"Do you wish to get well?" Jesus asks.

"Sir, I have no man to put me into the pool when the water is stirred up," the man answers.

"Get up," Jesus tells him, "pick up your pallet and walk."

Immediately this man—who hasn't taken a step in nearly four decades, and perhaps never—rises to his feet and begins walking. Can you imagine the scene? The cheering, the high-fiving, the mouths hanging open in amazement, the man shouting with joy. Nothing could dampen a day like this, right?

Wrong! The religious "police" are on duty, and they notice this once-crippled man carrying his pallet—on the Sabbath. They confront him about his transgression.

In his defense he tells them, "He who made me well was the one who said to me, 'Pick up your pallet and walk.'"

"Who told you to take up your pallet and walk?"

The man looks around, but in all the excitement, Jesus has slipped away unseen.

Soon afterward the man encounters Jesus in the temple. Then he's able to come and tell the authorities who it was that healed him.

Given a name, the religious police can now hunt down the law-breaker responsible for this deed. To these guys even a life-changing deed isn't legal on the Sabbath. Work is work, after all, even if it's good work. Not only had Jesus broken the rules by healing someone, but He'd also encouraged the healed guy to break the rules by telling him to carry his pallet.

When questioned by these accusers, Jesus explains: "My Father is working … and I Myself am working" (5:17). As if He isn't in enough hot water already, calling God His own Father makes the religious police crazy. They want to kill Him. Healing cripples on the Sabbath is bad enough, and pallet-carrying is worse. But blasphemy? Unforgivable!

Jesus attempts to clarify: "The Son can do nothing of Himself, unless it is something He sees the Father doing; for whatever the Father does, these things the Son also does in like manner" (5:19). Allow me some license to paraphrase: Jesus is saying, "I was walking by the pool and noticed a man who was lame. My Father whispered in My ear, 'Let's heal him, Son.' Because My Father and I work together, I said, 'Great! Let's do it.'"

In *Experiencing God,* Henry Blackaby uses this story in John 5 to point out the importance of our joining the Father wherever He's at work—in contrast to our notion of "dreaming great dreams for God" that we then ask Him to bless. It's not our place to ask God to join *us*; our responsibility is to move and join *Him*.

Jesus models this perspective when He states, "The Son can do nothing of Himself, unless it is something He sees the Father doing" (5:19). When I worked my way through *Experiencing God,* I got hung up on this statement. Could Jesus really do *nothing* of Himself? I'd always been taught that Jesus, while fully man, is also fully God. As God incarnate He was certainly able to heal a cripple without help from God the Father, wasn't He?

In the end it's an irrelevant question, because the Father and Son act as one. Why do they act as one? Jesus explains: "For the Father loves the Son, and shows Him all things that He Himself is doing" (5:20). The Father and Son work as They do, side by side, because of Their love for each other.

God calls you and me to join Him in His work so we can become better friends. God wants to "love on you"—so He says, "Join Me." He blesses us with His friendship, His companionship, His very presence, so He can whisper in our ears as we travel through life, "Let's share the good news of My Son with your neighbor," or "Let's write a check to meet that need," or "Let's show mercy to that person who's hurting."

Service that comes in response to the whisper of God is service filled with His power—power that's needed by both the servant and the served. This power flows from our friendship with God. What a blessing!

Blessing 2: God's Life-Shaping Influence

My boys, Kyle and Kirk, have always enjoyed sports. They began playing soccer, baseball, basketball, and football in organized leagues as soon as they were old enough to do so. Soccer and baseball came first, when they were about five. Basketball was added a couple of years later. Flag football started around fourth grade. Tackle football followed that. They moved from sport to sport, season to season, throughout the year.

And I would move with them, not simply as a cheering parent, but in many cases as a coach. I'd originally intended to pursue a career in coaching when I headed for college. The Lord later changed the desire of my heart regarding my career, but He didn't remove my love for sports or my desire to coach. Fortunately for me, when my sons started playing sports, the opportunity to coach presented itself.

Soccer came first. I know little about soccer and knew even less back then. But how hard is it to yell, "Kick it!" to a swarm of five-year-olds? But as they got older and strategy became critical, I became a cheering soccer parent.

On the other hand, baseball, basketball, and football were the sports of my childhood, and with those I coached the boys and their teams as long as possible, even lasting throughout Kirk's high school years in coaching football.

As I reflect on all the seasons, all the games, all the practices, all the team parties, a smile comes to my face. I've had a great time. It may sound selfish to put it that way, but I have. I've been so blessed through my involvement. We had some fantastic victories as well as some heartbreaking losses. We had championships seasons plus some "at least we had fun" seasons.

Most of all, my coaching has given me two great opportunities with regard to my own boys.

First, we've had time to hang out together. When most dads were dropping their kids off for practice, I stayed to lead practice. I didn't sit in the stands; I sat in the dugout or paced the sideline. I really enjoy hanging out with my kids (this includes my daughter, Karalyne). I found that being on the playing field and involved in the game with my boys gave me the opportunity to do more of life with them. My relationship with them benefited as a result. So it's not difficult for me to understand God's desire to do life with His children (Blessing 1).

Second, sports provided a wonderful framework from which to shape our boys as young men. For players as well as coaches, the athletic arena is a place where life lessons can be learned as character is shaped and tested. Qualities such as discipline, self-control, perseverance, and humility are required for success.

Without a work ethic an athlete will not reach his or her potential. Learning to rise above how you feel is essential. You may not feel like lifting weights or going to practice, but go anyway, because feelings don't dictate behavior. Do what's right in spite of how you feel.

Life comes with wins and losses; learn to handle both in God-honoring ways. Life isn't fair; don't expect it to be. Yes, the umpire made a bad call, but bad calls are a part of living in an imperfect world. The only one who never makes a bad call is God; put your trust in Him.

You learn too that it's imperative to respond appropriately to authority. And that cheating is completely unacceptable.

Playing on a team requires the building of relationships with all kinds of people. Learning to applaud the success of one while supporting the failure of another comes with the territory. Some people are more talented than others, but treat them all the same. Respect shouldn't be based on the ability to hit a baseball or make a basket or score a touchdown.

The list of lessons goes on and on. The athletic field has been a place of life-shaping influence.

God, as our heavenly Father, calls us to His playing field

with the same heart for His sons and daughters. Our involvement in the work of His Kingdom (His playing field) gives us the opportunity to hang out with Him (Blessing 1). As we do, we're further blessed by His influence on us as we submit to His "coaching." "For it is God who is at work in you, both to will and to work for His good pleasure" (Phil. 2:13). God is working *in* you, and He carries out that work while you carry out the work of the Kingdom.

Who benefits most from the teaching of God's Word, the hearer or the teacher? Whose heart is most uplifted in worship, the one who sings or the one out of whose heart the song originated? Those who go on a short-term mission trip soon learn that the experience affects them more than those they serve.

As we actively involve ourselves in God's purposes in our world, He shapes our character, our minds, our hearts, our values, our wills—our very beings. We become different people.

Statistics indicate that the average father spends less than three minutes a day in meaningful interaction with his children. Perhaps this is because their paths don't cross in common interests or activities. Though living in the same house, such fathers and their children live in different worlds. Similarly, when a believer fails to understand that life is to be spent in serving God's interests, he's in effect living in a different world than God is. Without the common interest of God's Kingdom and glory, such a believer misses out on the blessings of God's friendship and influence.

To have less than three minutes of meaningful interaction a day with our heavenly Father is a tragedy. To live life so absorbed with getting ahead in this world that one has little time, energy, or thought to give to the accomplishment of God's will is equally tragic. As Paul writes, "No soldier in active service entangles himself in the affairs of everyday life, so that he may please the one who enlisted him as a soldier" (2 Tim. 2:4).

When we're entangled in "everyday affairs" instead of laboring in God's Kingdom, the misfortune is not that His purposes won't be achieved; they will be. The tragedy is the blessings lost in the life of the believer who seeks first his or her *own* kingdom. Any worldly "blessings" achieved by such a focus are temporary and shallow compared to the blessings of God. We need His friendship, and we need His shaping influence.

Blessing 3: A Life Filled with Meaning and Purpose

The call to participate in the work of God is a call of deliverance. Our response to God's call frees us from a life of meaninglessness.

Armand Hammer, the former head of Occidental Petroleum, once said, "In order to succeed, a businessman has to have a love affair with money. That's why I'm such a brilliant businessman … money is my first, last, and only love." In contrast Jim Elliot wrote, "He is no fool who gives what he cannot keep to gain that which he cannot lose." To focus one's life in pursuit of the things of this world is ultimately meaningless. Armand Hammer's love affair came to an abrupt end, with no lasting value, when he died in 1990. While his pursuits brought temporal pleasure in this world, they provided no true sense of meaning. Jim Elliot, on the other hand, gained eternal reward, and the impact of his life on earth continues to this day, fifty years after his death. God calls us to a love affair that brings with it eternal value—and great meaning in *this* life too.

Several years ago, while living in Chicago, I had the opportunity to do ten days of teaching and consulting with several churches in Hawaii. While Hawaii in January was nice in itself, the highlight of the trip was the ministry that took place throughout those ten days. God seemed present at every involvement. I could feel His power at work. I sensed His wisdom being imparted through me. The teaching I presented was received with great affirmation. I went to bed each night with a heart full of satisfaction—a sense of His active grace enabling me to be faithful, fruitful, and fulfilled, and to make Him famous.

On my last Sunday there, after speaking at a church, one of the men attending the church invited me to go golfing with him that afternoon. At the risk of truly embarrassing myself (high handicap), I agreed.

Little did I know this man belonged to a country club in Honolulu that annually hosts a men's PGA Tour event—or that the professional tournament was taking place *that week*. The course was prepared for the pros coming to town. Sponsor tents were set up. Television towers were in position. JumboTrons were in place. A large leaderboard sat off the eighteenth green. We could feel the excitement in the air as everyone anticipated the days ahead. *This is pretty cool*, I remember thinking.

The course, as you would expect, was in immaculate condition. (I ended up seeing enough of it to know.) And the weather was typical Hawaii—eighty-two degrees, with a few scattered clouds dotting a vivid blue sky. Knowing I would be back in frigid, snowy Chicago the next morning, I tried to take in the beauty of it all.

The par-three seventh hole especially captured me, I recall. We were delayed on the tee, as the group ahead of us was still on the green. The hole, which sits parallel to the ocean, was to my left. The golf course lay to my right. Behind the course were the hillside homes of Honolulu. *Most people only dream of what I'm doing now*, I thought. This was the kind of thing people do on a once-in-a-lifetime vacation.

Those reflections were immediately followed by another series of thoughts: *This is fun, and I'm grateful for the opportunity—thank You, Lord!—but I'm glad my life wasn't built for moments like this. Given the choice between this and all the experiences of ministry over the last ten days, the choice would be a no-brainer.* The best this world has to offer cannot match the meaning, the fulfillment, and the joy that come when God releases His power through your life. *That* is what we were created for.

In Ephesians 2:10 we read, "For we are His workmanship, created in Christ Jesus for good works." We weren't created to have a love affair with money or the things it can buy. We can't find meaning or purpose there. Only in living out God's purposes can we find them.

God implanted the human soul with a longing for such meaning and purpose. He *made* us that way. And He calls us to His work so we may know the blessing of living a life that has value—real, *eternal* value.

Blessing 4: Personal Esteem

Take a trip to your local bookstore and ask an employee how many titles they carry in the self-esteem or self-improvement category. I did that recently. The customer service person led me to a section of the store where she estimated more than five hundred different titles on those topics were shelved.

Books on self-esteem and self-improvement obviously sell. Why? Apparently people want to feel better about themselves than they do. True esteem is something everyone wants, yet few seem to obtain.

In this regard we who know Jesus have a distinct advantage. We don't need to read the five hundred books on the store shelves. We only need to understand the significance of the first nine words in Ephesians 2:10: "For we are His workmanship, created in Christ Jesus." If you and I truly understood the weight of these words, we would never lack a sense of personal esteem.

MaryAnn and I had been married for only a couple of years when she suggested we go to Paris for a short vacation. Working as a flight attendant, she'd been there before and wanted us to go together. With her travel benefits the trip was very affordable.

So off to Paris we went, with plans to take in all the major "must experience" places in our few days there. One of them was the Louvre. Understand, I'm not an art museum kind of guy. Chicago, where I grew up, has a world-class art museum, but I've only seen it from the outside. I've never had a desire to go in. But this was Paris, and the Louvre is probably the most famous art museum in the world. I felt obligated to go. Having MaryAnn along slowed me down a bit, but I was still able to get in and out in less than an hour. (My apologies to those of you who truly appreciate great art.)

Inside the Louvre one of the must-sees is the famous painting *Mona Lisa*. As I stood in the back of a rather large room, I thought,

Well, there she is! Guards stood beside the painting, and red ropes prevented us from getting up close. Few works of art are valuable enough to receive such special treatment. In fact in that very room hung three larger paintings (each covered an entire wall), all of which I found to be more impressive than *Mona Lisa.* Yet *Mona Lisa,* I was told, is considered priceless. "What makes her so valuable?" I asked. The answer: "She was painted by Leonardo da Vinci." The painting itself wasn't so special; the person who created it was special.

Years later, as I sat pondering Ephesians 2:10, the Holy Spirit brought back to mind the day I saw *Mona Lisa,* and I sensed Him saying, "If that painting is priceless—an inanimate object hanging on a wall created by a man who's been dead five hundred years— what does that say for *your* value, as a living work of art created by the living God?"

The fact that "we are His workmanship, created in Christ Jesus," and that we were "purchased with His own blood" (Acts 20:28) makes us more than priceless. It's worth stopping for a moment to contemplate the profound nature of this truth. Here is the source of true self-esteem.

Of course, in communicating to us our value in His eyes, God didn't stop with those first nine words in Ephesians 2:10. The verse goes on to say we were created in Christ Jesus "for good works, which God prepared beforehand so that we should walk in them." Our value is not theoretical. It's not something to simply ponder; it's something for us to *experience.* God, in His grace, gives expression to our worth by creating us *for* something. We don't merely hang on a wall; we walk through life, and as we do, God leads us to good works, which we have the opportunity to carry out.

When we hear the whisper of God telling us we have an opportunity to engage in a good work, and we do it, we discover the meaning and purpose behind our lives. When we complete the work, we feel our value in displaying the mastery of the Artist who created both us and the good works themselves.

Think back to an occasion when God worked through you to make a difference in someone's life. How did you feel about yourself at the time? When you do a good work, what happens to your sense of self-esteem?

When we live to fulfill God's purposes, we not only put purpose into our lives, but we affirm our personal value. We *feel* the value that's truly ours in Christ.

Blessing 5: The Fellowship of Brothers and Sisters in Christ

Great experiences in life are made even greater when they're experienced with someone else. Climbing a mountain is much more fun with a friend. Completing a marathon is a thrill, but the thrill's even greater when we run alongside a family member or training partner. Who wants to celebrate being salesperson of the year by going out to dinner alone? A good movie or a great concert is always more entertaining with a comrade. Even a spectacular sunrise or sunset takes on greater beauty when someone else sees it with us.

This is also true in the difficult experiences of life. The heartache of defeat is lessened when shared with someone who truly understands. Walking through a trial is a bit easier when we have a shoulder to lean on. And fellow mourners ease the pain of losing a loved one.

True fellowship is one of the great blessings of life. Whether we're on the mountaintop or in the valley, life is better when fellowship is experienced. This truth is affirmed throughout the pages of the Bible, including here:

> Two are better than one because they have a good return for their labor. For if either of them falls, the one will lift up his companion. But woe to the one who falls when there is not another to lift him up. Furthermore, if two lie down together they keep warm, but how can one be warm alone? And if one can overpower him who is alone, two can resist him. A cord of three strands is not quickly torn apart. (Eccl. 4:9–12)

God's call for our participation in His work comes with the requirement that the work be done within a context of fellowship. We believers make up the "*body* of Christ"—a phrase that screams fellowship. How can we be a "body" without it? The body of Christ without fellowship is an oxymoron. Listen to Paul:

> But now God has placed the members, each one of them, in the body, just as He desired. If they were all one member, where would the body be? But now there are many members, but one body. And the eye cannot say to the hand, "I have no need of you"; or again the head to the feet, "I have no need of you." On the contrary, it is much truer that the members of the body which seem to be weaker

are necessary; and those members of the body which we deem less honorable, on these we bestow more abundant honor, and our less presentable members become much more presentable, whereas our more presentable members have no need of it. But God has so composed the body, giving more abundant honor to that member which lacked, so that there may be no division in the body, but that the members may have the same care for one another. And if one member suffers, all the members suffer with it; if one member is honored, all the members rejoice with it.

Now you are Christ's body, and individually members of it. (1 Cor. 12:18–27)

When we carry out the work of the Kingdom as the body of Christ, we receive the blessing of true fellowship. This is what God wants for us. If you're a parent, this is easy to understand; few things thrill parents' hearts more than seeing their children truly enjoying one another's company.

At the age of twenty, most of us are focused on *what* we're going to do with our lives. That choice, we believe, is critical to our happiness. And we hear from parents and other advisers, "Do something you'll enjoy."

But our happiness has another dimension that most of us don't understand until we're about forty. It's not *what* we do, but who we do it with. Isn't it true that a difficult job is much easier when you look forward to the relationships that come with it?

This simple truth became real to me many years ago on the

softball field. After college I played softball with a group of guys who were not only friends, but fellow soldiers in the work of the Kingdom, praying and serving together within the body of Christ. Once or twice a week, we played ball. Several times during the summer, we traveled together for a weekend tournament. What great memories I have of those times.

One day I received a phone call from an acquaintance on a different team from a different league. His team was short a player for their game that night, and he wanted to know if I could fill in. The game was taking place at the same field where my team played, so I agreed to come.

We won the game, and I played well. But afterward I walked to my car with a missing joy. Win or no win, it wasn't the same. I realized that, while I enjoyed playing softball, what I enjoyed even more was playing with my "brothers."

God understands this. He made us that way, because He wants His work carried out with the blessing of fellowship. Perhaps this explains why Jesus sent the seventy out two by two (Luke 10:1). Jesus could have reached twice as many cities if He'd sent them out as individuals—but they would have missed the blessing of fellowship.

Nowhere is the importance of fellowship more evident than in Paul's final letter, as he realizes his days on earth are nearing an end. He tells Timothy,

> Make every effort to come to me soon; for Demas, having loved this present world, has deserted me and gone to Thessalonica; Crescens has gone to Galatia, Titus to Dalmatia. Only Luke is with me. Pick up Mark and

bring him with you, for he is useful to me for service. But Tychicus I have sent to Ephesus. When you come bring the cloak which I left at Troas with Carpus, and the books, especially the parchments. Alexander the coppersmith did me much harm; the Lord will repay him according to his deeds. Be on guard against him yourself, for he vigorously opposed our teaching.

At my first defense no one supported me, but all deserted me; may it not be counted against them. But the Lord stood with me and strengthened me, so that through me the proclamation might be fully accomplished, and that all the Gentiles might hear; and I was rescued out of the lion's mouth. The Lord will rescue me from every evil deed, and will bring me safely to His heavenly kingdom; to Him be the glory forever and ever. Amen.

Greet Prisca and Aquila, and the household of Onesiphorus. Erastus remained at Corinth, but Trophimus I left sick at Miletus. Make every effort to come before winter. Eubulus greets you, also Pudens and Linus and Claudia and all the brethren.

The Lord be with your spirit. Grace be with you. (2 Tim. 4:9–22)

Nearing the end of his life, what does Paul have on his mind? *People!* And not people in general, but *individuals*. He mentions the names of more than a dozen people who stir his heart in some way. He speaks not only of the joy of true fellowship, but the pain of broken fellowship. His need and desire for fellowship are clear. Paul knows there's a blessing to be found in fellowship.

The implications of this truth in ministry are significant. No one should ever serve alone. When asked, "Do you need help?" never answer, "No, *I* can handle it." God wants us to experience the blessing of fellowship, especially in the trenches of ministry, because true fellowship is forged in the trenches.

Life's journey, with all its peaks and valleys, is always easier with the blessing of fellowship.

Blessing 6: The Joy of God

Would you like to experience a greater measure of joy? Silly question, right? Of course you would. We all would. The not-so-silly question is, *How can I?* The answer can seem elusive.

God doesn't want joy to be elusive. He wants it to be a moment-by-moment reality, every day of our lives. Paul lists joy as one of the nine characteristics that flow from the life of one filled with the Spirit (Gal. 5:22–23), so obviously joy is God's desire for us. He wants us to experience it even more than *we* do. And He tells us how!

"These things I have spoken to you," Jesus says, "so that My joy may be in you, and that your joy may be made full" (John 15:11). So what "things" had Jesus just spoken of? What is it that leads us to this joy Jesus wants us to experience to the fullest degree?

Here are the preceding verses:

> I am the true vine, and My Father is the vinedresser. Every branch in Me that does not bear fruit, He takes away; and every branch that bears fruit, He prunes it so that it may bear more fruit. You are already clean because of the word which I have spoken to you. Abide in Me, and I in you. As the branch cannot bear fruit of itself unless it abides in the vine, so neither can you unless you abide in Me. I am the vine, you are the branches; he who abides in Me and I in him, he bears much fruit, for apart from Me you can do nothing. If anyone does not abide in Me, he is thrown away as a branch and dries up; and they gather them, and cast them into the fire and they are burned. If you abide in Me, and My words abide in you, ask whatever you wish, and it will be done for you. My Father is glorified by this, that you bear much fruit, and so prove to be My disciples. Just as the Father has loved Me, I have also loved you; abide in My love. If you keep My commandments, you will abide in My love; just as I have kept My Father's commandments and abide in His love. (John 15:1–10)

Again and again, He speaks of the importance of *abiding* in Him, as one friend with another. This is Blessing 1, the friendship of God. If we want joy, we must embrace God's abiding friendship and presence.

His presence then brings His influence to bear upon our lives—Blessing 2—and His influence *in* us leads to His influence *through* us. Jesus calls this "bearing fruit," which He repeatedly says is His will for us. He shapes us so we "may bear more fruit." As we do so, the Father is glorified and we prove ourselves to be Christ's disciples (15:8).

One blessing keeps leading to another. Through fruit-bearing we receive Blessing 3: Our lives take on meaning and purpose, and we realize our true and *individual* value. This is Blessing 4: We're personally affirmed.

And as we join with others in fellowship (Blessing 5) to do God's fruit-producing work, we come face-to-face with Blessing 6—*joy*. Remember the commendation given to the servants in the parable of the talents in Matthew 25? "Well done, good and faithful slave. You were faithful with a few things, I will put you in charge of many things; *enter into the joy of your master.*" As a result of being faithful and fruitful in their efforts, they entered into their master's joy.

Likewise we read that the seventy Jesus sent out to minister two by two "returned with joy" (Luke 10:17). As they carried out God's work and experienced His power in and through them, they responded, "Oh, what joy!"

If you want to multiply your joy, Jesus tells you how to do it: Abide in Him, and bear fruit to the glory of God. He wants to bless us with His joy, and once we receive it, we, as the body of Christ, become a source of joy to the world around us.

What's more magnetic in its appeal than joy? The unsaved world is hungry to experience such joy. So abide in Him, be faithful, bear fruit, and watch God pour out His joy on *you*.

The Importance of the Blessing Factor

Why is it so important for leaders to understand the blessing factor?

First, we need to understand it for our own benefit. As leaders we easily focus ourselves on what needs to be accomplished. Our to-do list cries out for attention. We have programs and events to design and lead, meetings to plan and conduct, presentations to prepare, crises to resolve, and people needing direction. The very nature of leadership means we're engaged in accomplishing an objective—usually several. But our eyes can become so fixed on these objectives that we lose sight of the One who provides what we need to reach them. We read the Bible only in preparation for our next teaching assignment. Our prayer times are characterized by "we talk, God listens," as if we need to inform Him of what we need and convince Him of the urgency involved. We allow our personal worth to be determined by the numerical success of our last event and the prospect of numerical success in our next event. Our fellowship with others is reduced to task accomplishment. All in all, life is busy and noisy, and we have a difficult time hearing the whisper of God informing us of His thoughts and plans.

As a leader you cannot lose sight of your place as a beneficiary of the blessing of God. You cannot steward a grace you haven't first received. You need to experience the blessing factor personally. Your ministry must always be a product of your relationship with Him.

Second, as a leader you need to see the vital and critical role you play in helping those you lead to experience the blessing factor. This is at the very heart and foundation of being an equipping leader.

Let me illustrate. Somewhere around the sixteen-year mark of Willow Creek's existence, some of us began noticing a "morale problem" among our volunteers. Volunteerism had always been one of the great strengths of the church; now something was changing. Ministries were losing volunteers at an unusually high rate. People indicated they were overextended and out of gas.

I asked Bruce Bugbee, the director of Network, to convene a number of focus groups made up of various kinds of volunteers to see what was happening. Several weeks later a small group of us from the staff came together to hear what Bruce had learned. As he made his list on the flip chart, the problem became clear.

I could summarize it in a single sentence: *People felt used.* They saw themselves as a means to an end. They put out more than they took in. There was a feeling among too many of them that their leaders were simply "using" them to accomplish ministry objectives. We'd become serving-focused instead of servant-focused. Under the pressure of getting things accomplished, too many of us leaders had succumbed to the mind-set of recruiting people to fill slots in order to fulfill responsibilities.

We have created a word for such a mind-set: "usery." It's antithetical to the heart of God. It's antithetical to the biblical definition and understanding of leadership, which is all about equipping. God is a giver, not a taker. He's interested in making deposits in His people, not withdrawals. God is not a "user."

I think of Paul's words: "For this purpose also I labor, striving according to His power, which mightily works within me" (Col. 1:29). God's power fueled Paul's labor. And with that power Paul was then able to "power" others—exactly as he indicates in the preceding verse: "We proclaim Him, admonishing every man and teaching every man with all wisdom, so that we may present every man complete in Christ." Paul the leader had an objective, and he labored to accomplish it. Where did the power for his labor come from? *God!*

The heart of God is to equip (bless) His people. As leaders who follow His example, we're to labor in equipping our followers to experience the blessings of God.

Summary

How do we get more of God's people to serve?

Help them experience the blessing factor. Help them see that it's God's desire to shower His blessings upon them as they carry out His work. Assist and equip them to experience His blessings.

Imagine with me what your church or ministry team would be like if every worker were experiencing the blessing factor as a result of their serving involvement. They would experience …

- friendship with God.
- His life-shaping influence.
- meaning and purpose.
- personal esteem.
- true fellowship.
- the joy of God.

So be servant-focused, not serving-focused. Blessed servants will eagerly carry out works of service.

Put more into them than you take out. Become a leader who helps those you lead to experience the blessings of God ... and I believe you'll be pleasantly surprised by the number of people who will step out of the stands and onto the playing field.

9

THE ZONE OF GOD'S ANOINTING

As a lifelong Chicago sports fan I had the thrill of watching Michael Jordan lead the Bulls to six NBA championships during the 1990s. This was uncharted territory for me and my fellow Chicago sports enthusiasts, having endured countless losing seasons with our other pro teams. Having the world's greatest basketball player on "our" team was bliss. Over the course of his career, he provided us with many unforgettable moments. Two of them stand out most to me.

The first came early in his career, when he scored sixty-three points against Larry Bird's Boston Celtics. It was one of those nights when everything Jordan put up went in. No matter who guarded him, no matter *how many* guarded him, it didn't matter; he was unstoppable. He was in what athletes call a "zone."

The second such moment occurred in an NBA finals game against the Portland Trail Blazers, when Jordan scored thirty-five points in the first half, including six three-pointers. While Jordan was a prolific scorer, he was never known as a great three-point shooter. But in this particular game he couldn't miss. After making his sixth three-pointer, he passed by the scorer's table, in front of the television camera, and gestured as if to say, "What can I say? I'm hot. I'm in a zone."

Athletes understand the zone—those rare times when everything they try works, when the game comes easy, when success seems automatic. For the basketball player the rim seems as big as the ocean. The baseball player sees the ball coming from the pitcher as though it were a beach ball. The golfer sees the cup as a bucket.

It's not often that an athlete is in a zone, but when it happens, it's fun to watch. I can only imagine how much more fun it is to experience.

I believe God has a "zone" experience awaiting everyone who serves Him. This zone is the place of His felt presence and manifest power in ministry. It's the place where He shows up in and through a believer's life and bestows His blessing on another.

Our family recently watched a television special on the life and ministry of Billy Graham. During a commercial break one of my children asked if I could explain the impact of Billy Graham.

"I think I can sum it up in two words," I said: "*God's anointing.*" Is there really any other explanation? God's anointing puts the believer in a place of faithful, fruitful, and fulfilling ministry— the zone. Dr. Graham and his team have operated in the zone of God's anointing, and there God has manifested His presence and power. As a result they have seen much fruit and experienced great joy.

Have you ever heard a believer say, "I was born to do what I'm doing now" or, "God made me for this"? Such sentiments reflect the place of God's anointing in ministry service. And when a believer ministers from the zone of God's anointing, it's fun to watch. And, I can personally say, even more fun to experience.

Thankfully the zone of God's anointing isn't limited to the likes of Billy Graham. God makes it available to every believer. God's desire is that we all discover it.

Finding the Zone

A home on a beautiful lake in the Colorado mountains provided a perfect setting for a two-and-a-half-day staff retreat. I'd been invited to join five pastors from Grace Church as they met to consider the church's future. With Sunday morning attendance between seven and eight hundred, the church facility was nearing capacity. The internal ministries were struggling to keep up with the Sunday worship attendance. The organizational structure was better suited for a church of two hundred than one of eight hundred. The senior pastor was overwhelmed with relational and organizational demands.

So this was a good time to consider what lay ahead and what changes, if any, they needed to make. They invited me to help them discern God's leading.

We spent the first couple of hours getting acquainted and evaluating the current state of affairs. The spirit among the five pastors was great. They clearly loved the Lord, one another, and the church God had called them to lead. I imagined that the people of the church loved them as well. But the church's future direction wasn't clear.

By the end of the first morning together, I had a strong sense that two of the pastors were serving in roles that didn't fit who God made them to be. They weren't in this zone of anointing I'm referring to. I also sensed that two others needed some adjustment to their current roles. While these two were in the "ballpark" of God's anointing, they weren't quite playing the right position.

Based on my discernment and experience, only one of five was serving in his zone. This isn't to say God was absent from the ministry of the other four; He wasn't. And it's not to say they produced no fruit; they did. It was just my impression that a greater anointing was available, and a greater anointing would mean greater faithfulness, fruitfulness, and fulfillment.

I suggested they take an hour or so individually to complete an assignment that I believed would prove helpful in charting the church's future. The assignment had three parts and went like this:

> *Part 1*—List what you believe to be your primary spiritual gifts. Then write a one- or two-sentence definition of each gift you list. [I wanted to know what they meant when they said they had the gift of teaching or evangelism or prophecy. Spiritual gifts are defined differently in different settings, so I wanted to make sure we all had a common language and understanding.]

> *Part 2*—Write a paragraph stating what you're most passionate about in ministry. What is it that really gets

your juices flowing? What turns your crank, keeps you awake at night? What or who do you feel deeply about? Is it children, youth, the disenfranchised? Are you passionate about teaching or evangelism or counseling? If you could focus all your serving in a particular direction, what would that direction be? I want to hear your passion, so write a paragraph that expresses your passion within ministry.

Part 3—For part 3, you'll need to hear from the Lord. Make sure you're in right standing with Him so the lines of communication are open. Then ask Him to bring back to your memory five ministry experiences over the past one or two years that reflect His presence and power at work through you. I want you to identify moments in ministry service after which you said to yourself, "God was present in *that*," or, "I was designed by God to do *that*," or, "When I did *that*, God showed up." I'm looking for moments when you clearly sensed God's presence both in and through you. It doesn't matter how significant any of these moments were in terms of scope or size of impact. Whether you had this "anointed moment" with one person or a thousand persons is irrelevant. Just one thing matters: What were you doing when God showed up and displayed Himself through your life in an unmistakable way? Be prepared to share what happened. [What I was looking for here was what I call "anointed moments." Such moments produce fruit that is undeniable, bringing great fulfillment to the one anointed. They usually require relatively little energy on the part of the "anointed" one, because God's power is flowing.]

From the looks on their faces, I think the pastors questioned the value of this assignment. They wondered how this would prove helpful in charting the church's future. Nonetheless, they went along with it. (They really didn't have much choice, as they'd invited me to facilitate our time together.)

We reconvened in about ninety minutes, with the assignment completed. Each one of them spoke of his spiritual gifts, his passion, and his anointed moments. The exercise led to a true celebration and confirmation. Passion was easily identified and clearly felt. I don't recall any disagreement over spiritual gifts identification. I did a lot of listening, with a little inquiry along the way, for clarification.

Doug's Zone

One of those present was Doug, the youth pastor. Earlier, in our first session, I'd learned that the youth ministry averaged about thirty students in attendance. Considering the demographics of the community and the number of families in the church, thirty seemed awfully small for a church nearing eight hundred. The others greatly affirmed Doug; he had an obvious heart for God and students. So no one really understood why the ministry remained small compared to what it could have been.

After going through the three-part assignment I'd given, I too could see that Doug had a passion for students and a heart for discipleship. He loved to relate to students and build into their lives. In each of his five anointed moments, he mentioned the name of a student he'd built a relationship with. With great enthusiasm he spoke of how the Lord had used him to help nurture that student in his or her relationship with Christ. More than once he said, "I love to disciple students."

His number one "moment" was actually spread over three years, as he met weekly with a student to disciple him. This discipling relationship had borne great fruit in this young man's life, and Doug was thrilled to have been used of God.

All agreed that God clearly showed up through Doug's life when he was engaged in personal discipleship. As I listened, it became clear why there were just thirty students in the church's youth ministry. That's the number of students Doug *himself* was able to relate with to a significant degree. The youth ministry he was leading was built around his personal relationships with students, and thirty was his capacity.

I learned that the youth group was going on a retreat in a couple of weeks, and Doug would be in charge. When we took a short break, I pulled Doug aside and said, "I bet you're looking forward to this retreat being over."

The look on Doug's face showed that my comment struck a responsive chord. "That's exactly how I feel," he responded. "How did you know?"

"I led a youth ministry some years ago," I answered, "and I understand all that goes into leading a retreat—securing a facility, arranging transportation, planning a program. And kids get bored so easily and quickly that it's no small thing to keep them entertained for a full weekend. You probably had to line up a speaker and some special music, and you've had to collect money from the kids and manage a budget to make sure all the expenses are covered. Leading a group of high school students for a weekend takes a lot of planning and execution, not to mention administration—and it would be my guess, Doug, that you don't enjoy all that."

"I don't. Why *is* that? I'm a youth pastor. I should enjoy leading retreats."

"Doug, let me describe a different scenario for you. Imagine that on that same weekend you were instead taking four sixteen-year-old guys on a weekend getaway. You don't need a bus; they can fit in your car. No special facility, no program, no keynote speaker, no budget to administrate, just you and four guys hanging out for the weekend. How would you feel about that?"

"I'd love it! That's what I enjoy doing."

By this time Doug's mind was spinning. I could see by his expression that he wondered what I was trying to say. "Doug, you currently have a role in this church that calls for you to build and lead a large group. *Do* you want to build and lead a large group? Based on all you identified as you completed the assignment, where do you get the idea God wired you to build and lead large groups of people? You never even mentioned the word *group*. Based on what I've heard, I'd conclude that God shows up in your life and brings a blessing through you when you minister to students individually."

That's when Doug revealed that he'd been talking with his wife over the past few months about possibly returning to school to pursue a degree in counseling. "Do you think that makes sense for me?" he asked.

I responded, "I'm obviously not the Holy Spirit, and I don't want to pretend I know God's plans for your future. But it does seem to make sense that a relationally driven ministry will enable you to serve within the zone of God's anointing."

A few months later Doug left the staff of the church and enrolled in seminary to get his counseling degree. Around the same time, he launched a ministry designed to encourage father-son relationships. This passion was born out of Doug's relationship with his own father, which had been severed when he was twelve. Now reunited with his dad, he wanted to help other fathers and sons connect with one another. The ministry prospered for a season of two to three years.

But Doug eventually found himself, once again, building and leading an organization, and the business realities that come with running an organization took their toll. Doug was forced to set vocational ministry aside. He's now employed in the marketplace, endeavoring to honor the Lord there.

Several years have passed, and recently Doug and I spoke by phone. Once again we discussed the zone of God's anointing in his life. He still believes relational ministry is the zone for him. Being the CEO of an organization is clearly not. In the meantime Doug's love for the Lord continues to grow. God's pruning in his life is evident. He continues to see fruit being borne through disciple-making relationships.

Jim's Zone

Jim was the newest member of the Grace Church staff. A lawyer, he'd left his law practice six months earlier in cooperation with the Holy Spirit's leading and had come on board to provide much-needed administrative management and leadership. By title he was the church's business administrator. With a senior pastor (Andy), whose primary gifts were evangelism and shepherding, and an associate pastor (Lance), whose gifts were shepherding and mercy, the need for organizational leadership was obvious.

As Jim shared from his assignment, it was obvious to me he possessed the strongest wiring in the group for what I've called organization-building leadership. In relating his five "anointed moments" he never mentioned an individual name. Each of his moments revolved around a group of people whom he'd led in the accomplishment of a stated objective. Jim loved to build and lead teams. He was clearly motivated and gifted to mobilize others for the work of the Kingdom.

While he was fully capable of being the church's business administrator, such a position wasn't going to fully capitalize on all that God had wired Jim to contribute. This was a church in need of an "executive pastor" who would focus his energies on building an organization capable of moving the church to greater levels of fruitfulness. I saw Jim as God's man for this role.

During one of our breaks, I pulled aside the senior pastor, Andy, to get his take on what he was hearing. He believed his staff members were accurate in what they'd shared.

"And what about you, Andy?" I asked.

"I'm overwhelmed with trying to lead this church," he answered. "I'm *so* busy. I need to get back to evangelism, which I love to do. I want to phone people who are new to the church. I want to build into people's lives. I'm *not* an administrator. I don't *want* to manage all that I'm managing. What do you think I should do, Don?"

"I believe you need someone to take over the responsibilities associated with running the church. You need someone to lead the organization, someone who can help build and oversee the church's leadership team. You need a person to provide direction for the staff as they seek to lead their ministries. You need someone to give leadership to the business operations of the church and free you up to get back to what God has wired you to do—evangelism, shepherding, disciple-making."

"Where do I find such a person?"

"I believe he's already here."

Andy's facial expression registered surprise. "Who?"

"Jim."

"But Jim's a lawyer," Andy countered. "He's not ordained, and the role you just described would require an ordained minister."

I didn't know the denomination's rules and regulations concerning ordination in Andy's church, and I said so. But I added, "I still believe God has brought Jim on board here to provide the kind of organization-building leadership this church needs. What he has to offer will free you and Lance [the associate pastor] to do what both of you do best. I strongly encourage you to figure out a way to free Jim, and in turn yourself, to minister from the zone of God's anointing. Besides, God's anointing isn't based on ordination or education; it's based on gifting and character and godliness. Jim may not be seminary educated or officially 'ordained,' but from all I hear, he's a man of godly character whose gifting qualifies him for a role you and the church need as you head into the future."

To Andy's credit—and the church board's—they made the necessary adjustments, and Jim took on the role of executive pastor. To Jim's credit he went back to school part-time to pursue ministerial education. He eventually completed his master of divinity degree and is now officially ordained.

Both his ministry and the ministry of the church continue to flourish. Under Jim's leadership the church has received better guidance, and his new role allowed Andy the freedom to focus on his strong suit—relational ministry.

Lance's Zone

The responsibilities assigned to Lance, the associate pastor, included building and leading a number of ministries within the church. While Lance is a godly guy with a heart of gold who worked hard in his role, it wasn't really working. The ministries under his direction were struggling as the church grew numerically. On the other hand, Lance's personal ministry, based in relationships, was extremely strong. The trouble was, a church nearing eight hundred was too big to be geared around everyone's ability to have a personal relationship with him or Andy.

Over the next several months they placed most of the internal ministries under Jim's leadership, instead of Lance's. Even Lance was placed under Jim's leadership, and he was now freed up to teach, shepherd, and extend mercy to those in need. While this wasn't an easy transition for Lance at first (he was supposed to be the "number two pastor"), he eventually came to see the fruit and to experience the joy of operating within the zone of God's anointing. Even his physical health improved because of this adjustment to his role. He lives with far less stress and possesses even greater energy for ministry.

With these changes the future of Grace Church looked much brighter. Key leaders now served from the zone of God's anointing.

Your Assignment

What causes one person to produce much fruit, while someone else produces little? Why are some fulfilled to the point of bursting at the seams, but others minister with ongoing frustration? Why do some live with an affirming sense of being faithful, while others live with a sense of being a disappointment?

The answer doesn't lie in greater talent or gifting. Nor in personality or superior intelligence. God doesn't love and bless some more than others. More than anything else, some serve from the zone of God's anointing, while others do not.

Faithfulness, fruitfulness, and fulfillment are far more dependent on God's anointing than on anything we have in ourselves. If we think it's our great talent, or higher intelligence, or superior gifting, or charismatic personalities that truly make the difference, we foolishly and arrogantly deceive ourselves. If "success" in ministry were based on us, then we would only make ourselves "famous." But truly successful ministry makes *God* famous, because only by His anointing do we experience such success.

Do you want a ministry that flows from the zone of God's anointing?

God wants this for you even more than you do. So I have an assignment for you. Get away with God for a few hours. Make sure you're in right standing with Him so you can hear clearly; then ask Him to speak into your life as you complete this assignment:

> *Part 1*—List your primary spiritual gifts. Write a one- or two-sentence definition of each gift you list. Know what you mean when you say you have the gift of
>
> _____.
>
> *Part 2*—Write a paragraph describing your God-given passion in ministry. What turns your crank? What keeps you awake at night? What are you passionate about? What dimension of God's Kingdom is closest to your heart? Who in God's world tugs at your heart for His blessing?
>
> *Part 3*—Identify ten to twelve "anointed moments" in your ministry—the more recent, the better—when you sensed God at work through you, and explain in detail what occurred. Talk about service you rendered where God showed up. Give no thought to the significance of these moments. A phone conversation with one person, with God's anointing, is more important than speaking to ten thousand without it. These moments should cause you to say to yourself, "I was born to do this." "When I did this, God showed up."

After you complete the assignment, I encourage you to meet with two or three people who (1) love the Lord, (2) love you, (3) are secure enough to tell you the truth (rather than what you want to hear), and (4) are discerning and wise. Share the results of your assignment with them. Discuss any adjustments that could be made to your current ministry role to increase your experience within the zone of God's anointing. (Hint: If you've correctly identified your gifts and passion, they'll be reflected in your "anointed moments." You'll see certain patterns in those moments that affirm what God has equipped you to do.)

The goal in the end is to live an anointed life. Imagine what life would be like if its entirety were ordered in such a way that you lived daily in the zone of God's anointing. Seeing it in someone else's life is wonderful enough; imagine seeing it in your own!

As a leader, your job is to help those you lead to discover the zone of God's anointing in their life and ministry. The fruit of such leadership will speak for itself. As a leader you can give no greater gift to someone you lead.

I'd like to think that finding the zone of God's anointing is always as easy as I just described. However, experience tells me otherwise. Barriers exist to finding the zone, and genuine obstacles prevent God's people from experiencing faithful, fruitful, and fulfilling ministry that makes God famous.

Overcoming theses barriers begins with identifying them. Once identified, you can take steps to remove them from your path.

Barrier 1: Ignorance

Recall again Paul's words in 1 Corinthians 12:1: "Now concerning spiritual gifts, brethren, I do not want you to be unaware." Paraphrased: Don't be ignorant concerning spiritual gifts.

I grew up attending a strong Bible-teaching church, for which I'm grateful. Church attendance consisted of two hours each Sunday morning, one hour of Sunday school and one of worship. Our family returned most Sunday evenings for another hour of worship. During my grade school years I attended Boys Brigade on Monday nights. In junior high I went to Wednesday evening youth group. In all of this, the Bible was front and center.

But in spite of this background, I don't recall hearing a word about spiritual gifts until my freshman year of college. Perhaps because of sickness, vacation, or playing hooky, I just missed those Sundays when spiritual gifts were covered. I don't know, but somehow, I left for college ignorant on the topic. When I did receive teaching on the gifts, it struck me as revolutionary. The application of this teaching has had a profound effect on the course of my life.

While spiritual gifts have received much greater attention over the past twenty years, the number of believers, even leaders, who are ignorant concerning their spiritual gifts still astounds me. Your spiritual gifts represent the place of God's power in your serving, so you cannot afford to be ignorant. Do whatever it takes to get "in the know." Then do whatever it takes to align your service with the gifts God has given you.

Barrier 2: Neglect

A class session I was teaching on spiritual gifts was to begin in ten minutes. I sat in the back of the room, looking over my notes, as people began to file in.

"Don, can I talk with you for a moment?" Earl asked me. Well into his sixties, Earl was a long-term member and patriarch in the church. "I just don't buy all this stuff about spiritual gifts," he told me. "Serving is a matter of the heart. Find a place of need, and get involved helping out. Over the years I've tried to demonstrate a servant's heart. I've taught Sunday school, been on the missions committee, sung in the choir, served as a deacon, helped with the youth, held babies in the nursery, participated on the prayer team, worked in men's ministry—I've tried to help out *wherever* a need existed. All this focus and specialization based on giftedness, I just don't buy it. 'Find a need and serve to meet it'—that's my motto. I think the church would be far better off if we just all had a servant's heart."

I could obviously see that Earl felt strongly about what he'd just said.

"I wholeheartedly agree," I told him. "That's where it begins, Earl. Without a servant's heart nothing happens as it should." But then I respectfully asked Earl if I could "push back" on his comments a bit, and he agreed.

"I didn't come up with the concept of spiritual gifts, Earl; God did. As you probably remember from class, spiritual gifts are spoken of in Romans, 1 Corinthians, Ephesians, and 1 Peter. The subject isn't buried in some remote passage in a minor letter. It's front and center in the primary New Testament writings concerning how the church is to operate."

By now class was about to begin, so I encouraged Earl to go to the passages I'd outlined and ask God to show him the role of spiritual gifts in the life of the church. I applauded Earl for his courage in coming forward to express his thoughts. I also affirmed his servant's heart and thanked him for all he'd done to serve the church.

As he began to walk away, I stopped him and said, "Earl, I think I know your spiritual gift."

The expression on his face visibly changed, as if to say, "You do?"

"I think you have the gift of helps. From what you just stated, it's clear God has given you a heart to help wherever a need exists. I'm glad you're here today, because I'm going to talk about the gift of helps, or *service*, as it's sometimes called."

I don't think Earl really had a struggle with the concept of gifts. I think he was struggling with *how* he was gifted. None of the gifts I'd spoken about during the first two weeks of class rang a bell for him. He was feeling left out. But that morning he discovered that God had *not* left him out. The body of Christ needs people like him, people with a call to *help out* wherever help is needed.

As I travel to many churches and ministries that are "in the know" concerning spiritual gifts, I can see that ignorance isn't the problem; neglect is. They just don't believe in the absolute necessity of ministry based on giftedness and anointing. Their motto is "Find a need and meet it." In other words, "If you're willing, we can use you. If the task or ministry fits your gift, great; if not, no big deal."

While having a servant's heart is always necessary, that heart in combination with God's anointing is the source of ministry that makes God famous. I encourage you to read and meditate on the passages about how the body of Christ is to function, and about spiritual gifts in particular. May God increase your conviction so you settle for nothing less than anointed ministry.

Barrier 3: Lack of Self-Awareness

"I don't have the spiritual gift of evangelism." Those words came from Tom, the senior pastor of a church I was coaching. "I have a *passion* for evangelism," he told me, "but not a gift."

But as I met and interviewed the fifteen key leaders in the life of Tom's church, including both paid staff and lay elders, they all said, "Tom is an evangelist." His passion for evangelism was unmistakable. By his own admission evangelism was his *top* passion. It seemed to make its way into most every sermon he delivered. Yet in spite of the overwhelming affirmation of those closest to him, Tom stuck to his guns: "I don't have that gift."

"But evangelism is your primary passion," I insisted. "Its fruit is obvious in your ministry. Your preaching strongly emphasizes it. And everyone around you can see it. Are you still sticking to your story that you don't have the gift of evangelism?"

He wouldn't budge. He never did.

After years of coaching leaders, I've learned that the most difficult people to work with are those who are deceived about themselves. The pastor who believes he's a gifted teacher, in spite of his spiritually undernourished congregation, is tough to coach. So is one who thinks he has the gift of leadership even though the ministry lacks a strategy, and the congregation lacks a vision and a clear sense of direction.

We often see ourselves as more than we really are, or as who we *want* to be rather than who we truly are. We have blind spots, so we need others to help us see the truth about ourselves. We need to be secure enough to invite them to critique us.

Self-awareness about our gifting is critical. It's a sign of spiritual, mental, and emotional health, and if we're to find our way to the zone of God's anointing, we must first reach the zone of truth concerning who we are. Coming to a place of truth and contentment with one's own makeup is a wonderfully freeing thing.

Barrier 4: Ego

Human nature, or "the flesh" as the Bible calls it, is powerful. The apostle Paul often speaks of the power of the flesh and the war taking place between the flesh and the spirit. He writes this about his own struggle:

> I know that nothing good lives in me, that is, in my sinful nature. For I have the desire to do what is good, but I cannot carry it out. For what I do is not the good I want to do; no, the evil I do not want to do— this I keep on doing. (Rom. 7:18–19 NIV)

Our flesh—our egos in particular—can get in the way of serving in God's anointed zone. Earlier I spoke of Lance, an associate pastor who struggled with a transition that placed him under the supervision of Jim, a newly positioned executive pastor. Lance was seminary trained and ordained by his denomination; now he was reporting to someone ten years younger, not seminary educated, and not ordained. Worse, his new boss had been on staff for only six months. Lance was suddenly demoted from number two in the organization's hierarchy to number three, and many of the ministries for which he'd been responsible had been taken from him and given to Jim.

THE ZONE OF GOD'S ANOINTING

This was a real blow to Lance's ego. It challenged his level of self-awareness as he came to grips with his true gifting for ministry. In honesty Lance would tell you he battled his ego for several months. Thankfully he overcame the desires of his flesh and made a successful transition in his role—and found the zone of God's anointing in his ministry. In a recent conversation he told me of the joy and renewed energy he's experiencing in ministry. In addition his physical health, which had been declining, is better than it has been in years.

Our egos always take note of who's where on the organizational ladder. We know who's in leadership and who's not. Our egos also notice titles, credentials, and education. The very title "senior pastor" serves to stroke the ego, as it speaks more of a person's position in the organization than it does his or her contribution.

With regard to ego, we need to say what Paul does: "Wretched man that I am! Who will set me free from the body of this death?" (Rom. 7:24). We need to be freed from the delusion that one's position in the organization is more important than God's anointing. This is egotism, a trap set by our flesh, and "the mind set on the flesh is death, but the mind set on the Spirit is life and peace" (Rom. 8:6).

An inflated ego leads to bondage, so put your ego to death and trust God's anointing instead. Then you'll discover "life and peace."

Barrier 5: The Expectations of Others

My friend Steve was an elder in a church that was searching for a new pastor. Steve called to see if I could help.

A couple of days later, I received a two-page job description and character profile that spelled out exactly what the church wanted in a senior pastor. As I read it through, noting their expectations, I found myself wanting a nap. I was exhausted just reading it.

I called Steve back. He was a friend, so I could get right to the bottom line.

"Thanks for the job description, Steve. I've read it thoroughly. Now let me summarize my thoughts in one sentence: The apostle Paul isn't available, and even if he were, he wouldn't be qualified."

"That bad?" Steve asked.

"That bad! Based on your profile, Steve, your new senior pastor would need to be a prayer warrior, a mentor, an equipper, a teacher/communicator, a mobilizer, a visionary, an innovator, a risk taker, a manager, an evangelist, a representative to the community, an administrator, a financier, a change agent, a theologian, a fundraiser, a team builder, a strategic thinker, and a negotiator—all with a heart of submission and a great sense of humor!"

In addition to all that, they expected this pastor to preach a minimum of forty Sundays a year and provide key oversight and participation in Wednesday night worship and teaching. Of course they also wanted him to have a great marriage and raise outstanding children who loved Jesus and the work of His Kingdom. And I'm summarizing only a third of what filled those two pages!

"How could any one person be anointed of God to do and be all that?" I asked Steve. "If there were such a person, the rest of us wouldn't have a role to play."

Thankfully Steve and his fellow elders made major adjustments to their job description. They found their senior pastor, and he and the church are flourishing.

Kevin is the pastor of a young church with about two hundred in Sunday attendance. He asked me, "What should my associate pastor be doing?"

"Whatever God has equipped him to do," I answered. "We don't shape people to fit jobs; we shape jobs to fit people." Thankfully Kevin allowed his associate to fill a role that matched who God had made him to be.

We can and should expect people to do what God has equipped (anointed) them to do, and we should free them from expectations that take them clearly outside their anointed zones. Whether you're a paid staff person or a member of the laity, be careful of expectations that take you consistently outside God's anointing. God will provide others to fulfill those expectations.

I've lost count of the pastors I've coached who are ministering under a load of expectations that remove them from the zone of God's anointing. The consequences are crushing to them and their families.

Barrier 6: Institutionalism

Institutionalism is defined in one dictionary as "an emphasis on organization at the expense of other factors."

In the church one of the factors that often gets overlooked for the sake of adherence to institutional organization is the anointing of God. How ironic! What could possibly be more important than God's anointing in the life of a God-centered institution?

Go back to my conversation with Andy, the senior pastor I wrote about earlier in this chapter. When I told him I thought Jim was God's man for the role of executive pastor, he replied that Jim was a lawyer, not an ordained pastor. While Jim's transition to executive pastor eventually took place, institutionalism almost prevented a move that God was clearly behind.

How often do we limit what a "layperson" can do in ministry just because he or she is not a "pastor" (seminary educated and ordained)?

Recently, after delivering a Sunday morning message at a church, I led in the celebration of Communion. Following the service, a woman approached me, wanting to know if I was ordained by her denomination. When I said no, she told me she was "personally offended" that I'd led Communion, a role reserved for those who were ordained.

"God didn't invent denominations; man did; God didn't design ordination either; man did. Do you think Peter and the other apostles—and all the people who administered Communion in the book of Acts, for that matter—were ordained?" That's what I *wanted* to say. Thank the Lord, I didn't.

While this seems like an extreme example, that reaction is much more common than we like to admit. One of the great blessings of being involved with Willow Creek is the fact that no such institutionalism existed. The church didn't place limitations on God's people based on institutional rules and regulations. The only limitations were those imposed by God Himself through His Word. Godly character and affirmed gifting were far more valued than any educational or licensing credential, and were the basis for the privilege of leadership.

The vast majority of Willow Creek's paid staff came out of the marketplace. Laypeople (I dislike that prefix *lay*; it sounds so passive and lame) are ministers. They're called "for the work of service, to the building up of the body of Christ" (Eph. 4:12). While proper education certainly has its place, it should never be more valued than the anointing of God on someone's life.

When our ministry institutions, be they church or parachurch, prevent God's people from ministering from the zone of His anointing, they become a stumbling block. They're guilty of what Paul warns against: "holding to a form of godliness, although they have denied its power" (2 Tim. 3:5). He concludes that verse with strong language: "Avoid such men as these." No spiritual institution can afford to deny the power of the Spirit.

Every church or parachurch ministry exists as an organization to help God's people carry out His work for His glory. May we never allow tradition or institutional rules and regulations to stifle the flow of God's anointing in someone's life. Instead may our organizations strive to release the power of His anointing in each and every child of God.

Barrier 7: Entanglements

In 2 Timothy 2:4, Paul writes, "No soldier in active service entangles himself in the affairs of everyday life, so that he may please the one who enlisted him as a soldier." Everyday life can be entangling, especially for those employed in the marketplace. While we are to do all work "as to the Lord" (Eph. 6:7–8), the demands of the world of trade can be consuming. It's hard to keep one eye on heaven when your job requires two eyes on earth. How easy it is to become consumed with the here and now of the everyday world. The power of money, the currency of the marketplace, is especially alluring. Finding the zone of God's anointing becomes a side issue. But there's no such thing as being a Christian "on the side."

Sometimes we get so entangled with everyday affairs that living in the zone isn't even on the radar. On Sundays our hearts are stirred, but by Monday morning that stirring is a distant memory.

Entanglements come in many forms, including hobbies, relationships, possessions, and leisure—all good. But even good things become bad when they prevent us from living in the zone of God's anointing.

I've often thought that God led me to ministry as a career simply because He knew I needed to be on a short leash. I easily get entangled in the "affairs of everyday life." But no matter how appealing, rewarding, or enjoyable an entanglement may be, it will never equal the satisfaction of living under God's anointing.

Summary

Every serious athlete understands the thrill of playing in a zone. The game is never more fun than when everything you do seems to work.

What causes an athlete to find the zone is a mystery. It just happens—though not often enough for most athletes, unfortunately. If only the ability to play in a zone could be bottled and purchased!

The zone of God's anointing is every bit as thrilling. And the good news is, finding it isn't a mystery; it's a spiritual reality. It doesn't need to be purchased; God did all the necessary purchasing. And it's not limited to a special few, or the "professionals." It's available to anyone who knows Jesus as Savior and has a heart to live for Him. From there it's just a matter of cooperation with the Holy Spirit.

If you don't know your spiritual gifts and haven't discerned your center of passion, take steps to find out. (See the resources listed in the back of this book.) If anyone tries to tell you these things don't matter, don't listen. And beware of your blind spots as well as your ego, which will do more to put you in bondage than they will to set you free.

Make sure you live under the expectations that God places upon you. You'll never lack the power to fulfill His expectations. Avoid institutionalism, which speaks more of religiosity than it does true spirituality. And beware of those involvements that seek to entangle you, thereby preventing you from enjoying true success.

God's will is that you live an anointed life.

10

TRANSFORMING CONSUMERS
INTO CONTRIBUTORS

What do you consider your church's three greatest strengths? That's
a question I often ask during the course of my involvement with a
leadership team.

The answers I've received over the years vary greatly: *Our teachers ... music ... children's ministry ... youth ministry ...
single-adult fellowship ... missions program ... warmth and friendli-
ness ... sense of family ... Sunday morning service ... evangelism ...
prayer ... worship ... community service ... facilities ... giving....*
The list goes on. Sometimes these answers come quickly and easily
with a united voice of agreement. In other cases I hear more uncer-
tainty and diversity of opinion. But whatever the case, the answers
tell me a great deal about (1) the church's values, (2) the strengths of
its key leaders, and most of all, (3) where the Holy Spirit is moving.

Around Willow Creek's tenth anniversary our leadership
asked itself this very question. One answer came unanimously

and without delay: "The serving of our body" (volunteerism). One of the great strengths of Willow Creek Community Church was undoubtedly the army of believers who were engaged in the work of service. Their impact in the life and work of the church could not be overstated.

Shouldn't this be the case in every church? After all, what is the church if not an army of believers doing the work of service? This is central to what we're to be and do.

God expects *every* believer to participate in the "work of service, to the building up of the body of Christ" (Eph. 4:12). A church that fails to see *every* believer as a minister is failing to recognize what God Himself considers important.

And shouldn't "the serving of our body" be one of the primary strengths of *every* church's key leaders? After all, "equipping the saints for the work of service" is the essence of biblical leadership. Leadership that fails to equip the saints for service is not biblical leadership. The effectiveness of every leader in the church is ultimately measured by "the serving of our body."

Most importantly, shouldn't the serving of every believer be a sign of where the Holy Spirit is moving? After all, this is what the Holy Spirit does. It's the Spirit who distributes spiritual gifts "to each one individually" (1 Cor. 12:11), and as these gifts are put to use, the Holy Spirit's presence and power are displayed "for the common good" (12:7).

"The serving of our body" should be one of the three greatest strengths in every church.

If only it were as clear and easy as I just described. But it's not. One of the greatest challenges facing the leadership of every church is that of turning consumers into contributors. People are by nature

TRANSFORMING CONSUMERS INTO CONTRIBUTORS

consumers. Becoming contributors calls for a work of the Holy Spirit. Although "the serving of our body" was a strength at Willow Creek, it was still far from what it could have been. In the best of churches, serving involvement falls short.

I'm currently involved with a church leadership team that has put great effort into "equipping the saints for the work of service." I've been encouraged and impressed by the level of serving involvement I see. Still, a recent survey in this church revealed that just 46 percent of the congregation is involved serving in the church. Given the fact that most churches function according to the 80/20 rule (20 percent of the people doing 80 percent of the work), 46 percent is pretty good. The leadership team can only imagine what their church would be like if 100 percent of the believers served.

So how do we change this reality? How do we meet the challenge of turning consumers into contributors? How do we grow the number of those fully engaged in the work of service?

While the answers are neither short nor easy, we need to understand and apply a few essential elements. In churches that identify "the serving of our body" as one of their greatest strengths, we find some common denominators of belief and practice that make an essential difference.

Let me run through four of these essentials.

Essential 1: A Belief in the Priesthood of All Believers

At the very foundation of any church with strong serving involvement is a deeply held belief in the priesthood of all believers. This belief is taught, modeled, and practiced. In fact this belief is taught, and taught, and taught, and then taught some more—a recurring theme in the church's teaching ministry.

I remember the fall, early in Willow Creek's history, when senior pastor Bill Hybels presented a teaching series titled "Serving Lessons" at the Wednesday night ("New Community") service. Week in and week out for four months, the church received instruction in how to serve. Bill hit serving from about every possible angle; he didn't want anyone to be in the dark or one bit confused about God's thoughts on this. While the message and series titles changed over the years, the basic content did not. Church leaders taught the biblical principles concerning the body of Christ repeatedly, and, therefore, the average believer understood those principles well.

In the mid '80s we added Bruce Bugbee to our staff for the express purpose of creating a vehicle to help the people of Willow Creek find a place of meaningful service. His efforts resulted in the formation of the Network Ministry. At the heart of it was the "Network Serving Seminar," a four-week interactive teaching program designed to help people find a place of gift-based, passion-driven service. We offered the seminar eleven times a year, and we *strongly encouraged* every believer to attend.

Through such ongoing teaching in multiple settings, the value of serving became a part of Willow Creek's DNA.

In addition to the teaching came modeling and practicing. Words aren't enough; people need to see the words lived out, just as Paul says: "For our gospel did not come to you in word only, but also in power and in the Holy Spirit and with full conviction; just as you know what kind of men we proved to be among you for your sake" (1 Thess. 1:5).

This teaching and modeling were reinforced by the circumstances under which Willow Creek began. For starters we made no distinctions based on pay, since we had no money to pay salaries. Every member of the "staff" was a volunteer. Second, no one had received formal ministry training. We had no seminary graduates, so we were all "laypeople." Titles like "pastor" were irrelevant. Third, the amount of work needing to be done required "all hands on deck." If the work of service had been left to only a few, the church would have folded.

The priesthood of all believers was not merely a biblical concept or a theory to us; it was a way of life. It was the only option, given our situation. Looking back, I can easily see the advantages of those circumstances.

Fortunately, as Willow Creek grew, the body of believers continued to play a major role in the church's development. They weren't merely supporters of "professional staff people." They were chief contributors. Although we valued formal education, we never held it above godly character, a strong relationship with Christ, and the application of one's spiritual gifts. We seldom used titles such as "pastor." We called each other by our first names, which was natural and served to reinforce the truth that we're all ministers.

Titles and labels like "pastor" serve to reinforce the distinction between professionals and laypeople. This distinction is something we should be undoing, not reinforcing.

Even with the church's rapid numerical growth, we never outgrew the need for "all hands on deck." And perhaps due to the fact that so many of our people came from non-church backgrounds, no one knew any other way. Participating in and contributing to the work of service was a normal and expected part of the Christian life. The priesthood of all believers was a way of life.

I would encourage you to gather your leadership team together and have an honest conversation around the following questions:

- What do we believe the phrase "the priesthood of all believers" to mean?

- What are we doing to teach, model, and practice the priesthood of all believers?

- What are we saying or doing to reinforce our belief in the priesthood of all believers?

- What are we saying or doing that undermines our belief in the priesthood of all believers?

- What practical steps can we take to make the biblical concept of the priesthood of all believers into a value embedded in the DNA of our church?

Essential 2: Leaders Who Function as Equippers

I'll say it again: *Leaders equip.* Show me a church where "the serving of our body" is a strength, and I'll show you a church where leaders function as equippers.

For the past nine or ten years, I've been invited to participate as a guest lecturer in a doctorate of ministry class at Trinity Evangelical Divinity School in suburban Chicago. Two or three times a year the students—mostly pastors—come to the school for a week of classes. Having already earned a seminary degree of some kind, most have pastored for several years and are returning to school with a real-world understanding of ministry. Many have told me, "In seminary I was trained for the work of serving, not for the work of equipping." The trenches of ministry have brought them face-to-face with their need for a different set of skills. They've discovered that their role requires them to build and lead an organization, and apart from equipping others to serve, they can't accomplish this work.

This challenge to equip has also affected how they teach. An army sergeant readying his troops for battle teaches differently than a college professor preparing his students for a test. Teaching for the purpose of provoking to action is different than teaching to inform. Most of these pastors now see that what their people need is not more information, but help with application.

There's a critical difference between a *trained server* and an *equipping leader*. While formal education is beginning to reflect an understanding of this difference, in the past it focused on training servers. Seminary students were taught to study, teach, counsel, minister to the sick, care for the hurting, distribute the sacraments, perform weddings, and conduct funerals. As a result the average pastor entered the pastorate as a "serving machine." If he or she remained in that role, the church grew around them and, in most cases, remained small as a result. Members of the congregation were allowed to function as consumers, since they were paying a trained professional to service their needs. Many pastors observed this model in their own church backgrounds and as a result, carried it on.

But as I've tried to point out, this model has one problem: It isn't biblical! And those who adhere to it will never be able to list "the serving of our body" as one of their church's greatest strengths.

What's the core problem? A pastor, filling a leadership position, is functioning primarily as a server (Eph. 4:12), not as an equipper (4:11).

In order to reshape this reality, three changes need to occur:

1. Those in leadership positions must begin to function as equippers. This can happen only if their Spirit-imparted gifts empower them to equip others. Those with primary spiritual gifts of a serving nature (such as mercy, helps, giving, hospitality, etc.) need to be repositioned as *servers*. In many cases this work of equipping will require some training. While equipping comes naturally to some, others must *learn* it—and they can, provided the person has gifts of an equipping nature.

2. Leaders must be held accountable for their effectiveness as equippers. Just because someone considers himself an equipper and fills a leadership position doesn't mean he is equipping. The proof, as they say, is in the pudding: Who has he equipped? Who is he equipping? What impact has this equipping had in the growth and development of the ministry?

3. Future leaders need to be identified and discipled. Paul instructed Timothy, "The things which you have heard from me in the presence of many witnesses, entrust these to faithful men, who will be able to teach others also" (2 Tim. 2:2). He didn't tell Timothy to find just any men; he said to find "faithful men." A leader has made an unwise investment in another person if that person is unable to pass on what he or she has learned to someone else. Identify people with equipping gifts who show forth the fruit of faithfulness.

Churches whose leaders understand the difference between *doing the work of ten* and *finding ten to do the work* will soon list "the serving of our body" as one of their greatest strengths.

Here are other questions that your leadership team should discuss openly:

- Who is each of us equipping? (List their names.)

- What are we doing to equip these individuals?

- What are we equipping them to do?

- How will we know when they've been equipped?

Essential 3: Gift-Based, Passion-Driven Ministry

During my freshman year of college, I received my first teaching on spiritual gifts. The concept absolutely fascinated me. I immediately wanted to know what my gifts were. I couldn't read through the definitions and descriptions of the different gifts fast enough.

In my initial reading I found that I had no connection whatsoever with some of the gifts. Others seemed to fit me to a tee. As I looked back at various serving involvements during my high school years, it became clear why I was so deeply motivated and seemingly "successful" with some of them: I had a "gift"— the Holy Spirit had given me a spiritual gift, and as I used it, God dispensed His power through my life. Understanding my gifts also made clear why certain involvements produced fruit. It seemed that all the good things I'd experienced in ministry service were linked in some way to the gifts of the Spirit in my life.

Thirty years have come and gone, and I'm more convinced than ever that what I just wrote is true. The use of our spiritual gifts in service makes all the difference. Therefore, to see the serving of the body as a primary strength in our churches, we must help people discover their giftedness. When God anoints our serving, everything changes. Motivation is no longer lacking; joy is no longer missing; results are no longer hard to find. God's power is expressed through a person's spiritual gifts.

Therefore the job of all leaders is to help their followers discover and use their gifts. This is at the heart of what it means to equip the saints for the work of service.

Our goal at Willow Creek was to help every believer discover his or her gifts, as well as a place of service allowing those gifts to be exercised. We believed that if every believer used his or her gifts, the church would be built as God wanted, and everyone would be better off. We didn't twist people's arms to serve. Neither did we make heartfelt pleas for people to "help out." We did make impassioned pleas that they get out of the stands so *they* could see how God had equipped them to play on His field. We strongly encouraged them to attend a Network serving seminar so that they could discover what God had created them to do in His church. We sought to create a culture that caused believers to feel as though they were missing something if they didn't know their spiritual gift. Hence the phrase "gift-based ministry."

That's the first half of the equation. The other half is passion.

Have you ever considered why the "Love Chapter" (1 Cor. 13)

is placed where it is? In light of the surrounding content, it almost seems like an interruption. Chapter 12 is about how the body of Christ is to operate based on spiritual gifts. Chapter 14 adds more about this. And sandwiched between them is chapter 13, focused on love. Wouldn't it have made more sense for chapter 14 to come on the heels of chapter 12?

But that's not how the Holy Spirit inspired Paul to write. The Love Chapter is exactly where the Spirit wanted it—in the middle. He wanted all God's people to know that love is the glue holding the body of Christ together, enabling the gifts to really work. In the final verse of chapter 13, Paul writes, "But now faith, hope, love, abide these three; but *the greatest of these is love.*" Without love, the body of Christ is not the body of Christ, and spiritual gifts exercised apart from love are useless. Love cements it all together. It's love that brings godly passion—and God's own presence—into the work of serving one another.

For many years at Willow Creek, we held an annual "Servants Retreat." It was a thirty-six-hour getaway in which the church's "serving core" came together to "stimulate one another to love and good deeds" (Heb. 10:24). At one of these retreats, I presented a teaching on gift-based, passion-driven service. When I came to the part about passion, I told them this:

"A number of you here believe that children's ministry is the most important ministry in the life of the church; none is more significant. As far as you're concerned, if the church did its job with children, almost everything else would fall into place."

A whole section of heads nodded in agreement.

"There are also a number of you here who believe much the same about youth ministry. You would explain how ministry to junior and senior high students is where lives really get turned over to Jesus. You know the statistics—85 percent of all those who come to Christ do so before the age of eighteen—so you're convinced the adolescent years are absolutely critical in shaping one's life."

Once again I could see several nodding heads. I even heard a couple of whistles of affirmation.

"Then there are those of you who believe the marriage-and-family ministry is the church's most vital endeavor, because of how it strengthens the home. If husbands and wives have God-honoring relationships, and moms and dads function as spiritual leaders, then the family can indeed be the backbone of not only the church, but all society."

More applause from another group. I kept going.

"Others of you would have us turn to Isaiah 61, the same passage Jesus quoted in Luke 4 when He first entered the synagogue in Nazareth and launched His public ministry: 'The Spirit of the LORD is upon Me, because He anointed Me to preach the gospel to the poor. He has sent Me to proclaim release to the captives, and recovery of sight to the blind, to set free those who are oppressed, to proclaim the favorable year of the LORD.' Based on this you would tell us that here we find what ministry is really most important, because God's heart beats most for the oppressed, the downtrodden, the poor, the sick, the hurting, the hopeless in this world."

At this point those serving in the pastoral care, counseling, and benevolence ministries were bobbing their heads, and I heard a few heartfelt *amens*. But I still had more to say.

"A number of you would try to end this whole debate by simply quoting Jesus, when He said, 'My house should be called a house of ...'" As I paused, shouts from the prayer team filled in the blank: "Prayer!"

"But," I continued, "the worship team will say, 'Not so fast!' You would say prayer is only a subset of the larger picture. The overarching and all-encompassing truth is that we do all things for the glory of God; therefore, *worship* should be the church's central ministry. Everything is done under the banner of worship."

As I continued, the responses from the various ministry teams were getting louder.

"Some of you, though, would remind us there's only *one* reason we're even still on the earth ... just *one* reason why Jesus hasn't returned ... *one reason* why the church is still in business. And that's the need for evangelism. You would quote 2 Peter 3:9 to prove it: 'The Lord is not slow about His promise, as some count slowness, but is patient toward you, not wishing for any to perish, but *for all to come to repentance.*' You'd like to see the entire body involved in evangelism to speed the return of Jesus."

Now the evangelists among us—not a quiet group to begin with—went crazy, making the most of this instant opportunity to do some recruiting.

I moved to missions and some other ministries in the church, then came to this:

"But of course, the reason we can quote what God thinks about all these ministries is that we've been taught His Word. Where would we be without that teaching? Isn't the Word of God at the foundation of everything in the church? Without the teaching of God's truth, none of us would understand His will for our lives."

I paused and could sense a collective *hmmm* from the crowd.

Finally I came to this conclusion:

"Actually one more ministry trumps all others. It's the ministry that helps us *be* the body of Christ, the ministry that helps all of us work in harmony, the one that ties us together and sees to it that everything I mentioned takes place as God desires.

"I'm referring, of course, to *my* ministry here at the church."

If they'd been holding tomatoes, I would have been pelted!

"My reason for walking through all these ministries was to make one simple point: *God has given each of us a different piece of His heart for His world.* When we bring each piece to the work of service, we collectively display the heart of God to one another and the world. No one of us has a heart big enough to contain the heart of God for humankind. No one of us has the time and energy to be involved in all that needs to take place. So God gives to each of us a passion—a *love,* if you will—for some dimension of His work."

I closed the session by asking this question: "What piece of God's heart do *you* carry? We need you to bring that piece to our church."

This is what I mean by the phrase "passion-driven." As I said in an earlier chapter, the church should be the most passion-filled organization on the planet. It can happen only when God's people serve in areas that reflect God's heart in each of them.

Believers become a force of incredible influence when they begin using their gifts in an area of passion. The leaders' job is to help them discover the piece of God's heart deeded to them. This will require some exploration, experimentation, and the affirmation of the Holy Spirit in times of prayer.

The days of "recruiting the warm and willing" should be over. The church needs to be characterized by *hot* and *impassioned* service.

Once people find their passion, we should hear them say, "I can't *not* do this. God has called me! To *not* do it would be an act of disobedience!" Get enough people thinking and talking like that, and "the serving of our body" will be a distinguishing strength in your church.

Now it's time to gather your leadership team again and have another heart-to-heart. This time, ask,

- What percentage of our people are engaged in gift-based, passion-driven service?

- What do we need to do to help our people discover their spiritual gifts?

- What must we do to help our people identify God's heart within them—their God-given passion?

- How can we help each of our people connect with a place of gift-based, passion-driven service?

Essential 4: The Opportunity to Experience Success

Earlier in this book I sought to define biblically what success in ministry looks like:

- Success is *being faithful*—doing what God has called you to do, using that which He has given you.

- Success is *bearing fruit*, both internally and externally (internally as the fruit of the Spirit characterizes who you are; externally as the gifts of the Spirit make you a person of Christlike influence).

- Success is *experiencing fulfillment*, entering into the joy of God (see Matt. 25:23) as you faithfully bear fruit out of that which God has given you.

- Success is *making God famous* by serving in "the strength which God supplies; so that in all things God may be glorified through Jesus Christ" (1 Peter 4:11). The aim and the result of faithful, fruitful, and fulfilling service is to make God famous.

Using this definition, God wants every child of His to be a success—and every child of God should *want* to be a success. This is the desire of every sincere believer. Whether you teach the Bible or sell cars for a living, success—biblically defined—is the goal. And the human heart will never know true purpose in life apart from this kind of success. It won't matter how much we accomplish in this world, or how much money we make, how many trophies we win, or how many awards we receive; we have been created to achieve success *in the eyes of God*. To this end the work of the church, and leaders in particular, is to help God's people be a success.

A church leader becomes a success when he or she equips the saints for "the work of service, to the building up of the body of Christ" (Eph. 4:12), and the saints become a success as they carry out this work. The leader focuses his efforts on equipping the servers; the servers focus on meeting needs in the body and in the world.

Unfortunately many leaders focus their attention on the needs instead of the servers, and as a result, see servers as a means to an end. I call this approach "usery," and it's the opposite of equipping. "Usery" *takes* something from someone in order to accomplish something else. Equipping *gives* something to someone for the purpose of building that person up. Leaders who focus their attention on accomplishing ministry objectives see the saints as the workforce to getting that done. They value a person's contribution more than they value the person. The saints become a means to an end. Again, "usery"—but no one wants to be used.

Let me emphasize again that God is not a "user" of people. He cares about *you*, not what you can do for Him. He doesn't even need us to do anything for Him. He calls us to His work in order to give *us* something: He pours forth His blessings, out of which we're able to bless others. We're then doubly blessed. God is a giver, not a taker.

Jesus modeled this in His relationship with His disciples. While He did a great deal of serving of the masses (healing, feeding, teaching, etc.), He focused His time and energy on equipping His disciples. They didn't see themselves as a means to Jesus' end; they saw *themselves* as the end. *They* were the objects of Christ's affection. Yes, Jesus had come to serve the whole world through the shedding of His blood, and taking that good news to the world would require a great expansion of effort. Yet He focused His ministry on building into a few, knowing they would take what they'd been given and pass it on to others.

They didn't even hear the Great Commission until the end of Jesus' days on earth. It was as if He said, "Oh, by the way, I want to give you an opportunity to participate in My Father's work." It was not until moments before His ascension that He said to them,

"Hey, remember the promise I spoke to you about earlier? About the Holy Spirit? Well, He's coming, and when He does, you will have the power to be My witnesses."

Earlier, following Jesus' resurrection, He turned three times to Peter—someone who three times had denied knowing Him—and asked, "Do you love Me?" Only when Peter declared, "Yes, I do love you," did Jesus tell him, "Tend My sheep" (John 21:15–17). Jesus was focused first on *Peter*, not on what Peter could do. If Jesus had been a "user," He would have let Peter go, considering him a failure and a wasted investment.

Leaders who lead as Jesus did will direct their attention and energy toward equipping these who follow them. This means investing in them, as Jesus did His disciples. Equipped saints will ultimately do the work of service to far greater degrees, and with much more "success" than *used* saints ever will. A leader with the heart of God is most deeply concerned with the success of those who follow him. Leaders who care most about their own success and the accomplishment of their goals and objectives end up using servers, not equipping them.

The bottom line: If you want a church where one of the greatest strengths is "the serving of our body," then commit yourself to helping every last one of them experience faithful, fruitful, and fulfilling service that makes God famous. The more believers you have who experience this kind of success, the greater the blessing your church will be to its own members and the surrounding world.

On a practical level, some suggestions:

- *Don't recruit people to fill slots.* Instead invite them to embrace a vision and make a valued contribution flowing from God's anointing. Help them see and understand the value of their contribution in the work of the church. Give them a vision not only for the ministry as a whole, but for *their* role in it. Perhaps you've heard the story of two stonecutters who were interviewed individually by a reporter. The reporter began each interview with "Tell me what you do." One stonecutter answered, "I cut stone." The other answered, "I'm helping build a cathedral." This second one had a vision. Imagine a church filled with cathedral builders. Call people to a vision of something greater than themselves, then call them to make a vital contribution toward its accomplishment.

- *Do all you can to make sure each servant's contribution is in keeping with his or her gifts and passion.* To help someone discover the zone of God's anointing is a gift that will alter the rest of that person's life.

- *Place each person in the context of a team.* Build a team and serve together. There's a world of difference between working *for* an organization as an individual and working *within* an organization as a team member. Sensing that you belong somewhere is a powerful feeling that every member of the body of Christ should experience.

Leading in this way will cause you to put more into those you lead than you ever take out. Being under your leadership will be a blessing to them and will end up bringing a blessing to others.

Summary

Every believer wants to be a part of a church where one of the three greatest strengths is "the serving of our body." This *can* be a reality.

Here's how:

- Teach, model, and practice the priesthood of all believers.
- Call and train leaders to function as equippers. Hold them accountable to focus their time and energy on helping those they lead to be a success.
- Help every believer discover a place of service characterized by the phrases "gift-based" and "passion-driven."
- Give every believer an opportunity to be faithful, bear fruit, experience fulfillment, and make God famous.

The result will be this:

> We all attain to the unity of the faith, and of the knowledge of the Son of God, to a mature man, to the measure of the stature which belongs to the fullness of Christ. As a result, we are no longer … children, tossed here and there by waves and carried about by every wind of doctrine, by the trickery of men, by craftiness in deceitful scheming; but speaking the truth in love, we are to grow up in all aspects into Him, who is the head, even Christ, from whom the whole body, being fitted and held together by what every joint supplies, according to the proper working of each individual

part, causes the growth of the body for the building up
of itself in love. (Eph. 4:13–16)

As a teacher and coach to leaders and organizations for the past
fifteen years, I've found that leaders are more strongly opposed to
the institutional model of ministry than anyone else. Pastors in particular want to see "the serving of our body" as one of the great
strengths of their church.

"But how do I get us there?" they ask.

You may be asking that as well. You want help in transforming
vision into action. You probably have a pretty good idea of what
you want to see happen. From reading 1 Corinthians 12, Ephesians
4, Romans 12, and Acts 2:42–47 about the body of Christ and how
it's to function, you've gained a vision for what you want the church
to be. Your question: "How do I make this vision a reality?"

That's what this book's final chapter is all about—*application*.
And because the results of applying the truth could significantly
change the course of your life and ministry, the next chapter just
may be the most important one in this book. So read on with an
eye toward application.…

PART THREE

Applying the Truth

11

EXPERIENCING LEADERSHIFT

Several years ago, during a stressful period of my life, I allowed pressures and responsibilities to crowd out physical exercise, and I was suffering the consequences. Though I was highly motivated to turn things around, I wasn't succeeding. I would do well for a few days or even a couple of weeks, but then the demands of life would once again take precedence.

Finally I called a friend who's a personal trainer and confessed my need for assistance. He agreed to help—*if* I agreed to work his program. I said yes.

The first thing he did was make me record everything I ate over the course of a week. This was both eye-opening and humbling. He also gave me a list of vitamins to take and a workbook to log my workout regimen. We met three times a week for six weeks, during which times he ran me through my workout.

I followed his program, and it worked. I was able to establish a routine that I was motivated to maintain. I implemented the changes I needed to make and achieved the results I desired because of my friend's assistance. Without him and his program (or something like it), I likely would have continued to struggle.

Desired change demands that we summon all the help we can get in order to be successful. Going it alone just doesn't work. Talk to a person who's successfully overcoming an addiction and you'll find that the key to his or her success is some kind of a *program*. Recovery programs such as Alcoholics Anonymous provide the guidance and support that are necessary for changing addictive behavior. Speak with people who have lost a lot of weight, and they'll inevitably talk about a specific diet or nutritional *program* they followed religiously. Similarly many people participate in a savings or investment *program* of some kind to prepare responsibly for retirement. It gives them the structure, guidance, and discipline they need to set aside income for the future.

Significant personal changes are always difficult; organizational changes are even harder, because of the fact that organizations are made up of so many people. For an organization to change, many people will have to experience the effects of change simultaneously.

I like this quote from King Whitney Jr.:

> Change has a considerable psychological impact on the human mind. To the fearful it is threatening because it means things may get worse. To the hopeful it is encouraging because things may get better. To the confident it is inspiring because the challenge exists to make things better.

The fearful, the hopeful, and the confident must all make their way to the same place regarding the desired change in your church or ministry. This presents a significant challenge for any leader.

The Final Step in Leading Change

In chapter 7, I mentioned four steps that help to provide the needed direction and motivation for desired change. We looked closely at three of them:

*Step 1—**Pray fervently** to access God's presence and power.* The motivation for change, and the energy needed to drive it, must come from the Holy Spirit. Regardless of how persuasive your leadership might be, without God's power, your efforts to drive change will fall short. Remember these words: "'Not by might nor by power, but by My Spirit,' says the LORD of hosts" (Zech. 4:6). Pray fervently!

*Step 2—**Teach God's Word** to make His will known.* The Word must be taught with clarity so God's will is clear. The desired change cannot be your will; it must be God's. As Paul wrote, "Be transformed by the renewing of your mind, so that you may prove what the will of God is" (Rom. 12:2). Teach the Word!

*Step 3—**Lead by example** to provide illustration.* When you provide examples that demonstrate the fruit of desired change, you illustrate the will of God in action. Paul understood the importance of this truth: "For our gospel did not come to you in word only, but also in power and in the Holy Spirit and with full conviction; *just as you know what kind of men we proved to be* *among you for your sake. You also became imitators of us and of the Lord"* (1 Thess. 1:5–6). Lead by example!

These steps will bring those with a heart to follow God to a place of *wanting* to make the journey toward change, because they understand this is His will for them.

But *how* will they get there? That's the final step:

*Step 4—**Create a vehicle** to assist application.* If people have to go it alone in pursuing change, the results will likely be disappointing. People need assistance. They need a vehicle of change, like the program my personal trainer had for me.

In 1986, Bruce Bugbee, Bill Hybels, and I created a vehicle we named *Network,* designed to transport individual believers to a place of faithful, fruitful, and fulfilling service that makes God famous. Since then more than a million believers have seen what the Bible says about serving in God's Kingdom. They've discovered their spiritual gifts and passions, and they've learned of serving opportunities that fit them. They've been led step-by-step through a discovery process enabling them to arrive at gift-based, passion-driven service.

Before *Network* (and now other vehicles like it), when it came to discovering one's gifts, passion, and a place to serve, most believers were on their own. The results were not pretty. Many believers never started. Many others quit because they became discouraged along the way. Only a few persevered to the end. This vehicle called *Network* provided the assistance so many of them needed.

Similarly another vehicle—a program called *Becoming a Contagious Christian*—has assisted many believers in their efforts with evangelism. Evangelism is an area of frustration, failure, and guilt for many of God's people. They want to be witnesses for Christ, effectively communicating the gospel message. They want to see their family and friends come into a personal relationship with Jesus. Yet many have found attempts at evangelism frustrating. They quickly conclude that the work of evangelism should be left to the professionals. The purpose of the vehicle *Becoming a Contagious Christian* was to equip the average believer with the skills for sharing Christ with others. In the last fifteen years thousands of believers have been assisted by *Becoming a Contagious Christian* and have come to see that evangelism is not a task to be feared but a lifestyle to be embraced.

Another excellent example of a helpful program is Crown Financial Ministries. The curriculum is designed to assist people with fulfilling God's will concerning their financial resources. Thousands have discovered God's truth about financial matters by participating in a Crown group. These people have received the assistance they needed to get their own financial houses in order.

Every program and ministry in the life of the church should be a vehicle for assisting with the application of God's will. Churches should design children's ministries to transport children to life in Jesus. Youth ministries should move students forward in their spiritual development. Small-group ministries should transport people to true fellowship with one another. Even the weekly worship service is a vehicle designed to lead people into an encounter with God.

When we view ministries and programs this way, they take on a new purpose—to take believers on a journey of life transformation. How different this kind of ministry is from a ministry that simply caters to the desires of consumers.

Viewing the church's various ministries as vehicles also affects the way we measure success. Our real goal is the application of God's truth in fulfillment of God's will. Hence, success is determined not by how many attend a given program, but by how many *apply* the truth that the program espouses. Life change comes with application, not attendance. Vehicles such as *Network, Becoming a Contagious Christian*, and Crown are designed to help change lives. While attending these programs is a step in the right direction, attendance alone accomplishes nothing. Change comes with application.

This helps explain why God has given us His church. Hebrews 10:24–25 says, "Let us consider how to stimulate one another to love and good deeds, not forsaking our own assembling together, as is the habit of some, but encouraging one another; and all the more as you see the day drawing near." As followers of Christ, if we're to make the needed changes in our lives and accomplish the things we should, we need to get with "the program." God didn't create us to go it alone. We need one another's assistance.

Wise King Solomon said, "If two lie down together they keep warm, but how can one be warm alone? And if one can overpower him who is alone, two can resist him. A cord of three strands is not quickly torn apart" (Eccl. 4:11–12). God established the church so none of us need go it alone. He designed the church to function in a way that we each receive the assistance required to become the person He wants us to be. As a result every dimension of church life—every ministry program, activity, service, and event—should serve as a vehicle to assist change.

A Vehicle for Experiencing Leadershift

If you're like most leaders, you've never been taught the skills required to change a culture. Directing change and managing the discomfort that inevitably accompanies any transition is a skill. You're probably well aware of the biblical concept of equipping, but what you want to know is, *How do I do it? How do I train others to do it?* For me to tell you "Just do it" would only increase your frustration. You need a vehicle.

If I were to end this book right here without giving you that vehicle, I would in effect be saying to you, "Go it alone; make the leadershift." I'd be guilty of doing to you what I've warned you not to do with others.

So I want to offer you that vehicle.

It's one that has been designed and built over the past decade to assist church and ministry leaders facing the need for personal and organizational changes like those you have read about in this book.

Experiencing LeaderShift Application Guide

The vehicle I'm referring to is called the *Experiencing LeaderShift Application Guide.* I've developed it in partnership with my friend Bruce Bugbee. After developing the Network Ministry in the late '80s, Bruce left the staff of Willow Creek in 1993 to help bring gift-based, passion-driven ministry to churches and ministries across the globe. The *Network* curriculum has now been translated into twelve languages and is currently being used by thousands of churches around the world to make such ministry a reality. Over the past ten years, Bruce and I have worked together to create a different kind of vehicle, with an even broader influence than *Network*.

We discovered separately that many churches and ministries have institutional beliefs and practices that prevent believers from engaging in gift-based, passion-driven ministry. While the *Network* curriculum was helping *individuals* discover their personal zones of God's anointing, it wasn't designed to produce the *organizational* change these ministries needed. Developing a church culture reflecting biblical beliefs and practices was a much broader and more difficult task.

The *Experiencing LeaderShift Application Guide* has been designed to help turn vision into action. Specifically it's intended to help you achieve the following objectives:

- Dramatically increase the effectiveness of existing leaders.
- Train leaders to function as equippers.
- Establish a biblical model of ministry (and move away from the institutional model).
- Create appropriate spans of care, so everyone is trained, valued, and nurtured.
- Make team ministry a way of life.
- Provide your church or ministry with a leadership development plan and strategy.
- Train leaders to "put more in than they take out" of those they lead.
- Give everyone in your church or ministry a vision of what

it means to be faithful, fruitful, and fulfilled in a ministry
that makes God famous.

- Raise up more leaders.

- Apply the instruction found in Ephesians 4:11–12 ... so
Ephesians 4:13–16 becomes a reality.

If you've read this book and thought, *Yes! This is what I want
for my life and ministry,* then I strongly encourage you to be inten-
tional about your application, just as James instructs us: "Prove
yourselves doers of the word, and not merely hearers who delude
themselves" (James 1:22). Don't be "a forgetful hearer but an effec-
tual doer," for this is the person who "will be blessed in what he
does" (1:25).

There's more—more of God and more fruit for His glory—
than many of us are currently experiencing. Why journey alone
when you can journey with others headed to the same place? Join
us in experiencing a leadershift.

Experiencing LeaderShift *Is a System*

Experiencing LeaderShift is a *system* composed of three separate
but linking resources that have been designed to transform vision
into action.

The first resource is this book, *Experiencing LeaderShift,* written
to cast a biblical vision for leadership in the body of Christ.

I've described above the second resource—The *Experiencing
LeaderShift Application Guide,* a step-by-step strategy to help leaders

function as God intended them to. This application guide can be studied on your own or along with other leaders.

The third and final resource is a six-session curriculum for ministry teams and small groups titled *Experiencing LeaderShift Together.* This third resource is designed to get everyone in the church or ministry on the same page, serving as a member of a team. Through *Experiencing LeaderShift Together,* the entire church or ministry experiences leadershift.

Proven Results

Following are remarks about the *Experiencing LeaderShift* system from a number of church and ministry leaders who have been utilizing it during its development:

In 1996 I met Don Cousins and was introduced to the *Experiencing LeaderShift* system. What a difference it has made! As executive director in a large United Methodist church, I have embedded this biblical DNA in more than one hundred staff and volunteer leaders over the past five years. The results speak for themselves: a dramatic increase in the effectiveness of existing leaders; greatly improved communication resulting from a common language for ministry; increased staff capacity as team leaders and trainers; practical help moving several staff and lay members to roles that better reflect their gifts; vastly improved systems that have increased the quantity and quality of volunteers; and, most important, a growing spiritual momentum as we have collectively aligned our ministry to God's plan of action for His church. I strongly encourage you to use the

Experiencing LeaderShift Application Guide for training your church's leadership.

—*Charlie Halley, executive director*
Covenant United Methodist Church, Greenville, North Carolina

The best thing about *Experiencing LeaderShift* is that it's so practical. It's like somebody finally put the wheels on the leadership-development car. I use it at every level of ministry, whether I'm working with our elder board, staff, or unpaid ministry team leaders. When I sit down with the people I oversee, I now have a tool that keeps us on track and asking the right questions about our ministry. There are a lot of "good" things we can do with our time and energy. *Experiencing LeaderShift* directs us to the things that really make a difference in identifying and developing leaders. We definitely believe that we're all in this together, working as a team to equip others for ministry.

—*Tom Cramer, associate pastor*
Geneva Presbyterian Church, Laguna Hills, California

Two things I especially like about *Experiencing LeaderShift*:

First, our experienced leaders started thinking outside the box, developed new enthusiasm for their responsibilities, and began to see a better picture of where their ministry fit into the overall scheme of things. This was the team who had approached this training thinking they were doing a great job (and they were!), so why tinker with what is working? Well, to a person they were stimulated to serve even more biblically.

Second, this training provides an entirely new way to view and do ministry that alleviates the anxiety inexperienced ministry leaders often have. In the place of that fear, a new energy develops to take on the challenge. You can see it in their countenance, hear it in their voices, and find it in their team members. Now ministry becomes contagious and energizes all who participate.

—Dave Carder, assistant pastor
First Evangelical Free Church, Fullerton, California

Experiencing LeaderShift is food for the mind and inspiration for the soul in helping us understand how the church can and should function. However, it is the *Application Guide* that is the conduit between inspiration and reality. In the *Application Guide* all your church leaders will be shown a step-by-step process that produces unity of purpose. No stone is left unturned, and ministry is broken down and then rebuilt in the model that produces spiritual fruit from our church ministries, its leaders, and the ministry servants who are mentored. In the end God is brought positive attention (glory) and the people of the church are built up!

—Barry Carroll, executive pastor
Horizon Christian Church, Valrico, Florida

We've been using *Experiencing LeaderShift* training and materials for over three years now and are very pleased with their impact on our ministry leaders. Our leaders enjoy the training class and feel equipped for their calling. We now have a common language for leadership that can be heard throughout the church, a way of talking about ministry strategy that bridges the gap between secular leadership theories and the language of biblical faith. We are committed to moving forward using the *Experiencing LeaderShift* materials and are looking forward to the continuing growth and development of this resource.

—*Pastor Kurt Helmcke and Elder Pam Bruning,*
North Creek Presbyterian Church, Mill Creek, Washington

BIBLIOGRAPHY

Blackaby, Henry T. *Experiencing God*, Nashville: Broadman & Holman, 1998.

"Church Facts and Pastoral Ministry" Ministry Resource Network, Moody Bible Institute. May 2000.

Hybels, Bill; Lee Strobel; Mark Mittelberg *Becoming a Contagious Christian; Communicating Your Faith in a Style that Fits You.* Grand Rapids, MI: Zondervan, 1995.

Lewis, Robert. *The Church of Irresistible Influence.* Grand Rapids, MI: Zondervan, 2001.

"Pastor Burnout: Combating A Churchwide Epidemic, As Featured on the *700 Club*, March 10, 1999," The 700 Club Fact Sheet, The Christian Broadcasting Network Inc. Virginia Beach, VA: 1999.

"The Pastorate: Troubled Lives" *The Atlanta Journal / The Atlanta Constitution,* October 19, 1996, Religion, R4.

"Strategic Renewal International." *Strategicrenewal.com,* December 12, 2005. http://strategicrenewal.com/.

"The Year's Most Intriguing Findings, From Barna Research Studies," The Barna Group. December 17, 2001. *http://Barna.org/.*

ADDITIONAL RESOURCES FOR EXPERIENCING LEADERSHIFT

Printed Materials

Network
Bruce Bugbee and Don Cousins, Zondervan
- Leader's Guide
- Participant's Guide
- DVD Drama Vignettes
- CD PowerPoint, User's Guide, Coach's Guide

Available in Spanish and many other languages

What You Do Best in the Body of Christ
Bruce Bugbee, Zondervan
Available in Spanish and many other languages

Discover Your Spiritual Gifts the Network Way
Bruce Bugbee, Zondervan

Walking with God
Don Cousins and Judson Poling, Zondervan
Available in Spanish and many other languages

Listed materials can be ordered from Bruce Bugbee and Associates at 800-588-8833 or brucebugbee.com.

Don Cousins—individual coaching, ministry
consulting, training, and speaking
www.doncousins.org
616-396-9625
don.cousins@sbcglobal.net

Bruce Bugbee & Associates—available for leadership assessments,
training and ministry consulting
www.brucebugbee.com
800-588-8833
staff@brucebugbee.com